Faces and Places
Cooks Mills, PA

A History of Cooks Mills, PA

Edgar Stallings

Dick DeVore

COOKS MILL, PENNSYLVANIA

Cooks Mills, also known as Pleasant Valley, was named in honor of a Mr. Cook who was reported to have rebuilt the Old DeVore Mill. The old DeVore Mill was constructed by Mr. Cornelius DeVore who also operated a distillery in the area as well. At one time, Cooks Mills had its own post office and Express and Freight Station.

Cook's Mill - In southern part of Londonderry Township, on the Pittsburg Division of B. O. RR and on the Bedford Division of P. R.R., has one store, grist mill and ten dwellings (in 1900). It is located 29 miles southeast of Bedford.

Faces and Places Cooks Mills, PA
Mountain Story Teller Publications
Copyright © 2014, by Dick DeVore
All rights reserved. No part of this book may be reproduced or transmitted in any form or by any means without written permission from the author.

ISBN (978-1495485046)

Forward

This begins book number two in the Faces and Places Series. This book will serve to explore the creation of a small community located near the State Line in Pennsylvania. Cooks Mills finds itself steeped in rich history from the early days of the settling of Bedford County. It would become home to Cornelius DeVore and this would serve as catalyst for the continued expansion of the community. Through the construction of rail service through the community it was then able to connect with other communities from Bedford to Cumberland.

This book is centered around the story entitled Going Home which was written by Mr. Edgar Stallings detailing his life growing up in this rural community. Through grateful contribution of his story, the contributions of others, and a little historical research, a collection of unique facts and features have been collected to tell this story.

As always with any historical account, we try to present the facts as we know them and allow the reader to make their own interpretation of those facts. If we differ in opinion on those facts, Mountain Story Teller Publications would love to hear from you to collect your knowledge.

I hope you enjoy this book as much as we have enjoyed bringing it to you.

Dick DeVore

Table of Contents

Going Home!	Page 5
Memories of Anna Lee Stair	Page 23
Businesses	Page 25
Railroads	Page 41
Churches	Page 48
Schools	Page 55
Roads and Bridges	Page 59
People	Page 65
Cemeteries	Page 79
Homes and Farms	Page 86
News from the Past	Page 93
Special Thanks	Page 105

Going Home!

Written by Edgar Stallings

Today is Thursday Feb. 5, 1998. While lollygagging in the luxury of this 5009th day of retirement I ponder the thought and roll it over and over in my mind. Could I travel down that dimly marked memory lane back to where I was born? Could I journey down that path to my birth place? Could this octogenarian reminisce backwards 75 years to those early childhood years? Could this old codger live again those precious by-gone years? The answer comes quickly and clearly. I'll go for it! Come journey with me and share my excitement and enthusiasm. I'll do my very best to not intrude upon my teen years very far.

We'll begin our walk at the Cross Roads School one mile from my birth place. This will be a much traveled route, one mile from home to school with a seven years perfect attendance record. This is my school-Cross Roads or sometimes called Stringtown School. Want to go in with me?? Uh, oh, there's the bell! The second bell, got to get moving! Teacher stands at the outer doorway vigorously ringing the bell and excitedly encouraging us stragglers to get inside and to our assigned places! We go up concrete steps, through the outer doorway into the vestibule where boots are removed, through a second doorway into our classroom, boys turn left to walk to their cloakroom-girls turn right. We take off and hang up our outer clothing and put lunch boxes upon a shelf. We go to our assigned desks -two boys or two girls to each desk, except some pupils in grades 1, 2 or 3 must necessarily sit 3 to a desk in some classes. Eight or more rows of seats hold eight grades - a row for each grade. We kids all sit facing the teacher whose desk is near the front center with her back to the wall length blackboard. Behind us, the entire wall is large windows. As we sit in our desks, the right front corner holds the flag on a stand-the left corner holds a globe on a stand as well as a huge dictionary on its stand. Teacher's desk holds the only pencil sharpener. The right corner of our school room, above the blackboard are two large spikes which cradle the "board of correction". Teacher exercises this "board" most efficiently and quite often to unwilling recipients- with good results! On the left side of our classroom, sort of to the rear, sits the "pot belly" that provides heat in the winter time. The first three graders were seated closest to the heat. Class begins. Teacher calls for a moment of silence, then she or an older pupil read 10 verses from the Bible, followed by teacher's prayer, then the Pledge of Allegiance to our flag while standing with our hands over our heart. Next came roll call where we responded as our name was called out by Teacher. After the first few days of school, Teacher took roll call by looking up and down the rows of seats and noting the vacant seats to which we were assigned for the school term-unless-unless- teacher invited one of us privileged boys to come sit very close to her desk! Teacher always "invited" some of us boys to take the choice seat - never once did I see a girl sitting up real close to Teacher's desk! Do not understand why!

Teacher needs only a few steps to the right or to the left in order to go from class to class. We are not supposed to pay attention while a class, other than our own, is being taught- but that is almost impossible! Our School room always held 40 to 60 or more pupils. In this classroom Teacher rules, reigns, teaches, settles disagreements, administers swift punishment, encourages, consoles, dresses minor wounds, wipes tears, loves and is loved. Teacher keeps the potbellied stove burning during the winter months. She or he meets parents occasionally for reasons unknown to this kid.

Teacher assigns two older boys to hoist the American flag on the pole in the schoolyard every morning, taking it down every evening, carefully folding it and never allowing it to touch the ground! We will linger here at Cross Roads School for a time, meet Mr. George Cook, my first grade teacher. I have known him through many years, until his death. Meet Mr. Homer Bennett, my second grade teacher who I often spoke to in the evenings at Mrs. Shoemaker's where he boarded. I liked him. From school records, my third grade teacher was Mr. Joe Markey. I do not remember him, nothing at all. Next, Miss Mae Lybarger was my teacher, I liked her! She paid me $1.50 per month to build fire every morning before she arrived for school I knew her all through her lifetime until her death.

Then Miss Ruby Clapper taught for two years. Miss Clapper planned to go to France-so she taught us some French choruses which we really enjoyed singing. My last teacher at Cross Roads was Mrs. Blanche Wise. I knew her all her lifetime. I like all my teachers, except Mr. Markey has totally escaped my memory.

The last several years at Cross Roads School we studied reading, writing, arithmetic (the 3 R's), spelling (which I loved) geography, history, language, health, music and drawing. I love reading, spelling and arithmetic-could do without all the rest! I look forward eagerly for the upper grades Friday afternoon spelling bees. As a 5th grader I won most spelling bees "putting down the 6th, 7th and 8th graders". I won one spelling bee when I spelled the word ASAFETIDA which can also be spelled correctly, ASAFOETIDA. What a pleasant surprise it was in Feb. 2001 when Guy Hyre, a classmate at Cross Roads told my daughters, Marsha and Elizabeth about a spelling bee he remembered that I won, and the very word on which I won! I had forgotten that my winning caused quite a bit of consternation to my older class mates and especially my cousin Lloyd.

Each day, as needed, two older boys would take a bucket up the road a short distance on Mr. Billy Stairs' property and draw water from his spring. One dipper for all us kids! Teacher always had a personal collapsible drinking cup!

Games we play are "Andy Over" where a like number of kids get on each side of the school house. We hit or throw an inflated ball back and forth over the roof without ever allowing the ball to touch the ground. Each person allowing the ball to touch the ground must immediately step out of the game. The team having the most players when recess bell rings wins the game. We play "Kiss Ring", Hide and Seek, girls play "Jacks", and boys play ball all year-marbles in the spring. We have lots of fun at recess and at noontime playing games! The recess bell and the lunch time bell announcing time to go out on the playground was most welcome.

I went to school early and made fire in the pot belly stove-one year for Miss Lybarger-$1.50 monthly-one year for Miss Clapper at $1.50 monthly. The same year I also made and kept fire for Miss Harriet Shaffer in the new prefab building on the same school yard. Miss Shaffer had a furnace. I lost one of Miss Lybarger's $1.50 checks and had to wait one month for a replacement, it seemed like a lifetime! I have many more pleasant memories of Crossroads School and class mates, and one very sad memory when we all went to the Cooks Mills Methodist Chapel to see the little Burley girl laying in a fancy box-we were all very sad. There were other sad times, too when teacher said, "I won't be back next year" that was a sad time.

I remember anticipating county superintendent Mr. Lloyd Hinkle's visit once a year and looked forward eagerly to hearing his speech. I placed Mr. Hinkle on the same level as President Lincoln and his Gettysburg Address. Christmas, Easter and Thanksgiving we presented plays, recited poems, drew many pictures. Plays which were presented to the school first, and then to parents, grand-parents, and friends in the evening's social occasions. In the spring, May Day was a happy occasion. Washington and Lincoln birthdays-silhouettes, cherry tree, hatchet stories, crossing the Delaware, cutting down the cherry tree-reading by candle-light, splitting logs, drawing and coloring our art classics. The lady teachers were much like moms to us kids-wiping tears, cleaning scrapes and bruises, wiping noses, encouraging us to try harder, scolding, paddling, and hugging hurt ones.

I can recall most of my play-ground friends. There is one I will never forget. She is a scrawny little lady with large brown eyes, straight hair with bangs down over her forehead, she is shy, beautiful, with white teeth that glisten! Skinny but pretty, her name is Gladys and I feel a certain attraction to her although I am much older than she. We'll see!

Classmates here at Cross Roads are:

- The Burleys: Floyd, Raymond, Clyde, George, Charlotte & Dorothy
- The Scritchfields: Mildred, James, Bill & Jack
- The Clarks: John and Anna Lee
- The Phillips: Merle, Afton, Arthur, Winifred, Hayden
- The Phillips: James, John, Keith, Robert
- The Hyres: Lee & Guy
- The Llewelyns: Irma, Paul, Harry
- The Stairs: George, Rollan, Frances & Allen
- The Fichtners: Mae & Eileen
- The Logsdons: Leo, Robert, Gladys
- The Logsdons: Timothy
- The Millers: John, Ben, Sarah
- The Masons: David, Albert
- The Stallings: Jane, Robert, Roy
- The Daveys: Edith, John, Sallie
- The Lowerys: Virginia, Robert, VernadaJe
- The Cooks: Bruce, Nial
- The Sohns: Dorotherene
- The Poorbaughs: Laura with Iva
- The Clites: Alverna & Billy

It has been wonderful spending time at Cross Roads after all these years but I must move on if I ever hope to travel memory lane back to my birthplace one mile distant.

Close by our school a little widow lady lives alone- I must say hello to her before starting out homeward! Her name is Charity Witt, everyone calls her "Chat." She is a nice person. I carry in her coal, wood and kindling after school. Our visits are brief. For my labor there is every time a thin dime which I always pick up from on top of the lower window near the door as I exit. Never once did she hand me my dime but she often said "Don't forget" and I didn't! Well goodbye Mrs. Chat, it's been fun and rewarding filling your coal box and your wood box and running errands for you!

With some regret I leave behind this familiar spot in Londonderry Township in the southern portion of Bedford County, PA. We turn our focus homeward passing by the prefab school building that houses the overflow of pupils from Crossroads School. Shortly we come to a familiar wooden structure spanning Gladdens Run. The covered bridge! On hot summer days a boy could find cooling shade under its roof. A place of rest. Springtime the waters beneath it yielded frog eggs, tadpoles, minnies, crabs, turtles and fish as big as 5 inches long-even small whales galore! Water under that bridge was home to muskrats, mink, and weasels-good for trapping in the winter months and trading their pelts for dollars! That covered bridge was usually a very friendly place- but-if darkness came while traveling homeward after delivering my papers or doing chores for Mrs. Chat crossing that bridge was an adventure, a hair-raising adventure! You see, trolls lived under that bridge. In fact several families of trolls lived there-many times making the most God-awful shrieks and unfamiliar sounds! There are big trolls and little trolls. Anyone squealing could send this boy running fast as I could up the hill and away from the bridge. I never could see one of those trolls but I heard them many times in the late evenings, especially in winter time. Trolls really lived under that bridge, but, that's not the half of it! In the evenings, when it was dark approaching that bridge, I often heard the headless horseman's huff beats "clippety-clop, clippety-clop" racing across the covered bridge. When I was caught on the wrong side of the bridge and hearing the dreaded "clippety-clop, clippety-clop" I could only act

brave and make a dash toward the bridge and race across it as fast as my feet would take me and then continue running till I reached the top of the hill with the headless horseman far behind me! What a boy has to endure while making a few cents delivering papers or doing chores! Never did see that headless horseman or his horse but I heard him so he was there riding back and forth. That covered bridge was very friendly in daytime but really spooky after dark.

In the wintertime we took our sleds and bobsleds up on the hill behind the Chapel and rode down the hill past the Chapel onto the public road, down that hill onto the bridge and through the bridge if we had shoveled some snow onto the bridge beforehand! It was fun. Sometimes we Cooks Mills kids and the Stringtown kids gathered under the bridge to skate on the frozen stream. On several occasions we boys narrowly escaped prison terms just for "borrowing" some nice pine boards off the bridge to build fire while skating! Imagine that! We only pulled off a few boards! This kid must have walked across that covered bridge at least 5000 times in my pre-teen years. Goodbye covered bridge!

We mosey up the hill till we reach a large white rectangular building. The Cooks Mills Chapel-let's stop a while- six or seven concrete steps lead up to a door on either side of the building. This place is familiar since I walk past it every day on my way to and from school. Here in my first Sunday School class, Delilah prayed and then she told us about Jesus the first time I ever heard about Jesus! Delilah read Bible stories. She gave us pictures to color. We picked our crayons out of her basket of broken crayons, picking out the largest crayon of the color we wanted--all broken crayons! We sang some choruses, "Jesus Loves Me" and "This Little Light of Mine" others I've forgotten. The very best part of the day came when Delilah mysteriously pulled out of her apron the O.N.T. thread box! Inside the box were tickets with pictures of "Jesus", "The Good Shepherd" and Bible verses like "Jesus loves children" or "Let your light shine" or whatever! Each kid got a ticket and when we have enough tickets we can trade them in for a Bible book, a plaque or any gift we would choose. Delilah is a jovial person, however her sister Esther, my next teacher was rather stern and much more demanding. I learn to like her a lot because underneath her sternness was gentleness, besides she gave each of us new kids in her class a brand new box of crayons to use, no more broken pieces! I graduate (I was promoted against my will) next into Esther's sister Mary's class. I was getting older. Finally I was 'moved' into Mary's brother Thomas' class. Thomas teaches us older boys and the men at the same time. The Logsdon sisters and brother are my only teachers here in the Cooks Mills Chapel.

After delivering my papers in Stringtown, I stop at the Chapel and spend hours talking with Mr. Phil Lowery who was building the fires to heat the building for Sunday School and Church. Mr. "Phil" (Fillmore) was a kind person who seemed to enjoy talking with this kid. Mr. Phil is Sunday school Superintendent and tells me many Bible stories. Lessons I learn from Grandfather Stallings and Mr. Phil help me to build fires in the public schools when I am only 11, 12 or 13 years old. Thanks to those two fine gentlemen. Sunday School is an exciting time but some of these Bible stories are almost unbelievable, imagine, Daniel in the lion's den or three Hebrew boys in a fiery furnace, or old Elijah going up to Heaven in a chariot of fire, yet somehow I do believe them for they are read out of the Bible, which makes a difference, for the Bible is true. Another thing is the Flood that covered the whole earth! How could Will's Creek ever gets as high as Wills Mountain which Pop-Pop said was 1000 feet high? Impossible. Sunday School is often late starting-we must wait till Blanche, Mrs. Stair arrives to play the piano. We sing several songs and some choruses before Sunday School.

The Chapel is a pleasant place in summertime, what with picnics and festivals. At the picnics we have fun, games galore, and lots of good food, ice cream, cake, pies, lemonade, and a washtub full of ice and pop. Festivals are always in the evening-lots of playing games, the same as picnics, lots of older people talking and hollering at us kids to not be so loud! At our festivals people came from as far away as Ellerslie and Hyndman to buy ice cream, cakes, pies, sandwiches, and talk-mostly talk! Often times at our picnic there would be a greased pig for some lucky person to catch, if you can, and take it home as your prize! I never caught one, but I did get grease all over me and my clothes! At picnics we also had the greased pole with a one dollar bill fastened at the very top! Rollan Stair almost always climbed up there and snatched that prize! I always tried and always failed. I usually spend thirty-five cents at a festival-what with a bottle of pop 5 cents, a piece of cake 5 cents and an ice cream cone 5 cents or 10 cents, candy 5 cents, sandwich 10 cents. At the end of the festival kids and grown-ups would all join hands in a great big circle while someone played music or chanted like an auctioneer, we would all go round and round and round and when the music or the chanting stopped someone was at the lucky spot and won a cake to take home and enjoy! What fun. Oftentimes 3 or 4 lucky persons took cakes home!

In the Chapel we had Christmas plays, Easter cantatas, Easter services. I liked recitations-didn't care for parts in a play. No speaking parts! Singing in the kid's choir was good. I can still hear Prof. Watts "Tut tut tut and his wooden stick hitting the piano top or the alter rail after we goofed on some part or hit a wrong note, or whatever! We made many mistakes while practicing but on the big night we were usually perfect! At Christmas time when Sunday school ended, we would hear a

"Ho, ho, Ho" coming up the stairway from the basement. "Ho, ho, ho Merry Christmas to all" and soon a jolly old Santa would appear carrying a huge bag on his back. He would stand in front of the altar and as names were called out each kid went up front and eagerly accepted the gift of candy, nuts, oranges and a toy or two in a bag! What an exciting time! A gift at home too!

There was one very sad time at the Chapel when the little Burley girl lay in that fancy box and so many kids' crying. Grown-ups called that box a casket. Really, we must move along, leave behind the many pleasant memories, the sad ones too, turning our faces homeward again. Behind us are the Crossroad School, the covered bridge and the Chapel. Just a short distance away at the foot of the hill we see a gate on our left side. That gate blocks the entrance to a narrow rutted road that wends its way to "up on the hill." The little Burley girl was taken in her fancy box in a long, shiny, black car and left there "on the hill." They put the shiny box in a deep hole and we never saw the little Burley girl again. That was sad. Mother and Grandmother Stallings are "up on the hill" too so it's not a good place to visit.

Let's go back to the gate and travel on down the public road. We walk about 1/4 mile and we pass a large barn in the field to our right, a cluster of farm sheds, a smaller barn, corn crib, a spring house, and a large red brick home. This is my friend John's home, the George and Ella Clark home. John's older brother and younger sister Anna Lee live here. John is my bosom buddy. We spend lots of time together. We play baseball and softball, sometimes walk to school or Sunday school together. Although I probably make a nuisance of myself, many times as I walked up the yard toward the porch before I ever got on the porch from inside, I would hear that familiar welcoming sound. "Come on in." Ella's invitation to this kid coming to visit with John, play ball, get cream or milk, or straw for our bed "ticks" or chaff which we used to get grass seed for our back yard, or to listen to Amos and Andy on the radio, or to share in the large bowl of apples on the dinner table. George and Ella are very generous and most kind to this kid. However when George's plans for John's afternoon conflict with our planned ball game, Mr. Clark is not thought of too kindly! Hoeing corn or plowing corn is never as important as playing ball, but we were never able to persuade Mr. Clark! Not once! Mr. Clark's taking in hay always takes precedence over our planned activities.

In the evenings while enjoying freshly popped pop-corn as the magic hour of 8 approached, there must be complete silence for 15 minutes and that's not easy for us kids! But Amos and Andy must be heard! The squawking radios do not co-operate very well! Silence is the order of the day, no matter whose home we are in when the witching hour of 8 brings Amos and Andy. John I have great plans to become taxidermists. We took a home study correspondence course. We filled a large vat with deer hides, coon skins, and a brown pheasant. Eventually we finished the pheasant, glass eyes and all-a very crude masterpiece! Lumps and bumps where they were not supposed to be! John and I were permitted to place our large vat in their cellar with its 'pickling brew' in which we immersed our hides prior to mounting them! Springtime comes-summer comes- the hides are still in the vat in the cellar! Baseball becomes the order of the day! But one day, the usually gentle voice commands, "Get that vat out of my fruit cellar now" The "pickling brew" has ripened the hides to a stinking mass! The order of the day had changed! So we hauled it out far away from the home into the field! That ended our taxidermy career. We will never get our names and pictures in Hunting and Fishing magazine. Many pleasant memories are around this home.

Many of our baseball games were played in the Clark's barn yard. Cows also used the barnyard!

So, we always policed the plate before beginning to play ball. Many times on arriving home after a great ball game "Mom" said "You smell like cows" and we did! John kept our balls, bats, gloves, bases & catcher's mask at his home for convenience. Pleasant memories abound as I head for home.

Next door, James Clark with his wife Pearl and two sons Donald (Mac) and Willard live. These folks, too, are very kind and generous. Apples, pears, and grapes in season, all you can eat-free! Always felt welcome in this home. The boys were much older than I, we never play together. I did feel the sting of gravel many times. When I insisted on traveling to the Cooks Mills Dam, or to Stringtown with Mac and my cousin Lloyd Hartsock! I was too small. They did not want me! They threw gravel to discourage me! When I got too close! Once I succeeded in going along with them to the Cooks Mills Dam where they promptly threw me clothes and all off a 16 foot cliff into deep water! I learned to "swim" dog paddle very quickly. That was the first time I had ever been in deep water! This one lesson Mac and Lloyd taught me to love water- deep or shallow! Pearl and Jim are kind, generous persons. Jim would allow us to use "Bird" (horse) to pull large sycamore logs off the island near our home for fire wood. Pearl shares fruit in its season, apples, pears, cherries- sometimes fresh sometimes in pies! Pearl often told me. I have a nice picture of your mother up in the attic, someday I'll go up there, get it and give it to you". So far I haven't received it! Two apple trees in the Clark front yard dropped fruit onto the roadway. Passersby could pick up a nice bruised apple, cut out the bruise and enjoy a very delicious piece of fruit, free! In the fall, those apples were somehow changed into a large glass of sweet cider! Jim and Pearl are among my regular customers for the "Cumberland Daily News" and the Grit weekly magazine. They're good folks.

Moving on, next door we meet Mrs. Shoemaker and her deaf mute daughter Clara. We must visit here! Mrs. Shoemaker is a widow, a Pennsylvania Dutch person, kind, generous, poor, but rich enough for her or Clara to hand this kid a nickel or a dime after I had filled the wood box or the coal bin in the evening after school or on Saturdays! Summertime I pick cherries, plums, prunes and gather rhubarb and pick currants for Mrs. Shoemaker. In the fall, its grapes and later on pound apples with a long pole and a wire cage on the tip- never bruise an apple! For when stored for winter use it would rot and cause others in the basket to rot. Clara sometimes allows me to gather the eggs from the hen house at the rear of the lot. Mrs. Shoemaker has a wooden paling fence across the front of her property, a gate kept closed by a bucket of rocks attached to a chain. When the gate was open the bucket was lifted. When the gate was closed the bucket was lowered! I white washed that fence one time! Took me all day Saturday. Mrs. Shoemaker "boards" my second grade school teacher as well as the two Winter brothers who owned the construction company that was building Route 96 from Ellerslie to near Hyndman. The Winters owned steam shovels and caterpillars, and compressors and drills and dump trucks. They had a lot of workers building the concrete road. Many times, at Mrs. Shoemaker's I was invited to go into the basement and get a big dill pickle out of the crock, or with a dish and fork in hand, get a bowl of homemade sauerkraut! Yum, yum! Occasionally Mrs. Shoemaker hands me a nickel or dime but most of the times Mrs. Shoemaker would motion to Clara with some signs and sounds. Clara would go to the cupboard, get the coins out of a jar and with some strange sound and much fanfare, excitedly present me my nickel or dime! Mrs. Shoemaker's college professor son, Ross from Winston Salem, North Carolina visits each summer. Another son, Harvey from Philadelphia, Pa. visits more often. Mrs. Shoemaker's garden was always planted in either the "up sign or the down sign" according to the Hagerstown Almanac. Many times I delivered a basket of hops to Mrs. Shoemaker and a few days later Mom would give me a nickel or dime which I gave to Mrs. Shoemaker in exchange for a small bag of "rubs" Mom used those rubs when baking bread on Thursdays. How Mrs. Shoemaker changed those hops into "rubs" is a mystery -but she did!

The Winters brothers had a blacksmith working near Neffsville sharpening drill bits and making repairs to the road building equipment. In 1927 I asked him for a job and he said "No". I was 1 0 years olds then. I tried to get the water boy job too, but an older school mate got that job. He was twelve!

I must move on, so with the wave of my hand, its good-bye to Clara and her mom. I walk a short distance homeward and on the right side of the road, a lane leads to the Earl and Emma Emerick home with their four children. They soon leave here and move to Stringtown. In their place Ed and Minnie Lowery with their ten or more kids! I was never in their home but I walk to school with Pauline, Annabelle, JoAnn and Millard. The other Lowery kids are much older.

Close by the Lowery home is Uncle Roy and Aunt Myrtle Scritchfield's home with Mildred, Jim, Billy, Jack and later on Coleen. I walk to school with Mildred and Jim. Aunt Myrtle is one of my mother's four sisters. I love Uncle Roy and Aunt Myrtle but he is something else! He oftentimes told me "When you was born, you was so ugly, your Mother took one look at you and didn't know whether to laugh or cry" At first, I was kind of mad at him, but when Tommy Logsdon told us in Sunday School class at the Chapel "We are all made in the image of God". Well, that settled it for me. Let Uncle Roy have his good times. At this home we often play games, Hide and Seek, Cowboys and Indians. Our homemade slingshot or bows and arrows we used to try and pick off sparrows perched on the electric lines across the road in front of this home. We often walk to school together with other kids along the way. At Aunt Myrtle's, evenings were a pure delight- what with home make popcorn, plates of fudge, bowls of apples, doughnuts, taffy pulls and card games. Pulling taffy is a delight as well as a pain since it is so hot on our hands yet the end result is pure joy in our tummies. Sometimes we sit on the front porch swing and talk till time for us Stallings kids to get home. On the Fourth of July and other holidays, the Welshes and the Fichtners came and there was lots of excitement and lots of food. I must move along!

Next door is a little red house where Jessie and Mary Logsdon live with their little ones. We walk a short distance and on the left side of the road, at a sharp turn in the road, an old brick home is where Ike Madden lives. Ike is an aged, kind, well respected man by everyone, a retired paper hanger. Ike shuffles along the dusty road from neighbor to neighbor, his dusty white floppy canvas moccasins shuffling along- being better suited for bedroom use, than the roadway. That ever present shawl draped around his shoulders even in hot weather! Yet another white cloth wrapped around his neck which he uses often to wipe the right side of his face where cancer has eaten away part of his jaw. We kids are cautioned to never eat food offered to us by kind, generous Ike. Nor do older folks use the generous bundles of rhubarb they have received from Ike's gentle hands! Ike's front porch is cluttered with junk-at least I call it junk. Inside his home it's the same. A second reason for folks accepting Ike's rhubarb and then not ever using it was that folks believed Ike once a year cleaned the little building at the end of his lot, and put the contents on his rhubarb which accounted for the extra-large stalks! When Ike became ill, many times I carried warm meals that Mom had prepared for him, to his home and up the stairs to his loft where he lay on a bed. He always thanked me graciously. When Ike is taken "up on the hill" everyone in Cooks Mills loses a good friend. His house stands empty. Everyone misses him. Good-bye Ike.

Next door to Ike's house is where the Martz's live. William and Elizabeth, better known as "Will" and "Lizzie" to all in Cooks Mills. Both are very short, aged, and kind persons. I'm almost as tall as either of the Martz'. Will walks with crutches. I run a few errands for Lizzie, never receive money but always some cookies, a piece of blueberry, apple, peach or even raisin pie which I never ever refused! Each summer two lady relatives visited the Martz' home. They play guitar and a mandolin and sing beautiful songs. What a treat! In summertime they would perform on the front porch with lots of neighbors gathered in the front yard. Nice folks-Will and Lizzie. Will died and was taken "up on the hill". Lizzie lived alone and many times neighbors would see a lantern going up the field to the cemetery and hear a voice calling "Will, Will, come home, Will." Neighbors would go up in the field and guide Lizzie back home. Sometime later Lizzie too was taken "up on the hill". The house stood empty.

We pass by the next house and come to Joseph and Annie Emerick's home. These folks are aged, quiet, not very friendly to us kids, never unkind, but sort of stern. Annie smoked a corncob pipe which she often put in her apron pocket while it was lighted! Never did she catch her apron on fire! I visit the Emericks a few times- remember their poll parrot which cussed like a sailor. If I used those same words I would get my mouth washed with Octagon soap. Joe and Annie sort of stay to themselves most of the time. Annie's speech is shrill, almost a cackle. I guess because she's old. Joe and Annie were both carried "up on the hill".

On the opposite side of the road, on the large corner lot stands a huge building with the words L.1. Stallings General Merchandise printed in large letters across the front. This is my home away from home. This blue-gray two story building is a store, a ware room and a home-all in one. The ware room among other things, holds the instruments for the Town Band. In this home, I was told by my aunts, I spend most of my first thirteen years of life. When I am about five, I remember Grandmother Stallings (Mom-Mom) bringing sister Jane and brother Bob into the home where they lived until Mom-Mom died. Then Jane went to live with Aunt Ella and Bob went to live with Aunt Rhoda. My Aunt Myrtle tells me that little brother Roy was taken care of by Will and Nora Logsdon, until Dad married "Mom" and then he was returned to Dad and "Mom". Mom-Mom is old, tender, a take charge of things person. Her long hair is put up in a bun. She wears long black dresses all with either tiny pink or tiny white rose like flowers in the print. Pop-Pop is a small man, kind, firm, doting on us kids, almost bald- the result of diphtheria when he was sixteen. Memories flood this home. Bob lay on a cot in the corner of the living room near death with pneumonia. The room is unbearably hot from the fired up Heatrola. So hot it seemed hard to breathe but Bob is helped and survives. Mom-Mom is rushing about taking care of us kids, cooking, cleaning, baking, or whatever. Mom-Mom's table was always "set". When a meal was over, dishes were washed put back on the table ready for the next meal, and then the table was covered by a tablecloth that kept flies and fingers from leftover pies or cakes. Mom-Mom had to keep both the Heatrola and her cook stove fires going. Mom-Mom often hung her rugs on the clothesline and then beat them with a' fancy wire thing having a handle. She gets her water by walking across the back porch onto the well platform and then pumping the handle up and down till water fills her bucket. Mom-Mom prepares many meals for visitors. Mr. Broadwater, a traveling surveyor or Uncle Billy Cook, Aunt Val from Elk Garden and many of Pop-Pop's business friends whose names I never learn. Mom-Mom is very pretty-wears high shoes that are fastened with a button hook. I remember Mom-Mom laying in a fancy box in the parlor, a big black car out front, lots of people, now Mom-Mom is "up on the hill."

Pop-Pop looks like an ordinary person but don't you believe it! He runs a grocery store, he is the postmaster, the B&O station agent, the A.R. Express agent, Township auditor. In his store he sells jewelry, hardware, harness, farm tools, clothing, wash tubs, shoes, bolts of cloth, and you name it! The Pittsburgh Post-Gazette along with a crate or two of bread from Rockwood arrive on the morning train -still warm! The store becomes a waiting room for railroad passengers in the winter time because the railroad station is not heated. In return for this free service to railroad travelers each fall the railroad work train stops and with its clamshell, drops off 4 or 5 tons of anthracite coal. Pop-Pop covers this coal with sheets or tin and uses it to keep the pot belly stove red hot in the winter. Pop-Pop and I get along well. He never ever raises his voice. He never scolds me. He is very kind and gentle but firm. He is out of bed early. Fixes the fire in the Heatrola, starts breakfast, and then calls this kid to get up. He cooks his pot of coffee, makes toast, cooks oatmeal or two banty eggs for each of us fried in a skillet. We often have cooked prunes. Always there is jelly or apple sauce, marmalade or preserves to put on our toast. I drink milk or water, cocoa sometimes.

I am about 5 1/2 when Mother dies and about 6 1/2 when Mom-Mom dies. There are many blank spaces in my memory. After breakfast Pop-Pop has to stir up or start a new fire in the pot belly stove to have the store warm for the first customers when he opens the store. Together Pop-Pop and I fix sandwiches, put fruit and a couple cookies in my lunch box. So off I go on my one mile trek to school. Over the years I remember walking with sister Jane, brother Bob, little brother Roy, the Phillips kids (two families), the Masons, the Hyres, the Scritchfields, the Emericks, the Lowerys, the Clarks and the Bannicks (very faintly). I remember mouth battles and a few fisticuffs. This very day brother Roy is starting school. He walks with us and promptly finds water puddles to play in and gets hands and clothes dirty. Little brother Roy is called Junior by all of us. Well, we've spent the day in school. Starting home I do my usual chores along the way. Arriving home I walk into Pop-Pop's yard past the pitcher pump onto the back porch, open the door into the living room/dining room-a very large room with table and chairs in the center- the table already "set" covered by a table cloth, as is usual. Near one corner is the Heatrola- close to the door I entered is another door leading to the small kitchen with its 3 burner kerosene stove on which meals are heated. On another wall a door leads into the parlor which is used mostly for special visitors. On another wall, one door leads out into the store while the other door leads to the stairway to the bedrooms on the second floor. A very, very large room with a sloping ceiling from about 9 feet down to 4 feet. From this room I walk through a doorway into Pop-Pop's bedroom and out of his bedroom down the stairway into the parlor! This in my home away from home. My bed is in the Sloping ceiling room oftentimes sharing with Cousin Lloyd or Cousin Hazel and her husband "Moats". Coal trains rolled down the mountain past the house shaking it till it rattled but it never caused this kid to lose a minutes sleep. We ignored the rumbling noise and vibration. Lloyd came home from Lancaster with locks or giant dolls from places where he worked. The girls got the dolls. When Hazel came home for a while she cooked meals and bossed this kid. I never cared much for her bossing needless to say! Hazel cleans the house real good and she brings another husband "Wooz" home with her. He isn't much.

Pop-Pop's store has concrete steps in the front, leading to double doors, shuttered at night to prevent break-ins. Inside the store, on my right, is the large pot belly stove. In front of me on the counter sit three large rounded glass show cases-one for jewelry, one for cigars, one for candy! To the left of the jewelry case stood a large cabinet closed in the front, many cubby holes open in the rear, each holding mail. This is the Post Office! The B & 0 train brought a bag of mail which Pop-Pop sorted and placed in the proper cubby hole to be handed out to folks at their request. Pop-Pop also handled packages as the agent for the Railway Express Agency. Hidden from view, underneath the counter is a large safe with cash, stamps, money orders, jewelry and valuable papers. I am eleven or twelve when Pop-Pop gives me the combination to his safe. Above the safe, under the counter, was the money drawer which could be opened only by pressing the right combination of levers which were partly hidden. In front of the counter, in season, are 15 or more buckets of salt fish. Pop-Pop loves them- this kid hates fish. Period. A separate showcase holds paper, pencils, pens, ink, crayons, carbon paper, paint boxes, tablets, notebooks, school supplies. On top the counter stand 2 large rolls of wrapping paper, each with it's dispenser and blade to cut the proper length of wrapping. Close by is a smaller cutter which is used to cut picnic twist tobacco or cigar tips. From behind the counter, one need only walk through the doorway and into the living/dining room home. At the same place, the counter top folded upward to allow one to pass from behind the counter into the customer's area or vice versa. One needed this privacy to keep out the loafers who usually sat around the pot belly spitting tobacco juice toward the coal bucket and

missing most of the time! Behind the counter, on the wall was a large clock, beneath the clock a 3 drawer cupboard containing O.N.T. thread of every color imaginable. Beneath it is a large display of dyes. The shelves behind the counter hold shoes for the family, work clothes for all, dress clothes for men &boys, shirts, ties, trousers. Ladies dress bolts were on the counter and on the shelves behind the counter. At the far end of the counter a rounded glass display case holds longhorn cheese, underneath are boxes and buckets of candies, chocolate drops, jellies, hardtack, nigger babies, peppermints! Macaroni and spaghetti in their identifiable boxes, sugar and flour in 50 or 100 pound bags. Dried fruits in their 40 pound boxes. Chipso and Octagon soap in their familiar wrappings. 50 or 100 pound bags of Lima or soup beans. At the end of the store a door led to the ware room where musical instruments of the Cooks Mills band were stored. On the opposite wall we find hardware, coal buckets, shovels, and farm or home supplies of every sort. Pop-Pop has kegs of wooden shoe nails, slate boards, boxes of slate pencils, sarsaparillas to drink. Chicken wire, wire fencing, tools for farm or garden, rolls of barb wire, nails, staples, saws, pry bars- you name it! At the rear of the store stands a hog's head barrel full of fish. There are carpenter's tools, masonry tools, hunter's tools and fishermen's tools. Just across the road Pop-Pop had another large building where bulk items were kept. One very large tank of kerosene with its own pump. One large tank of motor oil with its own pump. Large cans of carbide, bags of fertilizers, and many large boxes of dry goods. Cousin Lloyd's Harley-Davidson was on its stand stored in this room while Lloyd was at work in Lancaster. Well this kid was cautioned to never get on that bike! But I did! And one day the bike overturned with this kid's legs pinned underneath the bike. I couldn't move. Gas was seeping out of the tank across the floor towards the large boxes of matches piled

3 or 4 feet deep. I screamed and hollered," Help, Help, Help" until a passerby came in and freed me, no worse for my terrifying experience! I really thought that when the gasoline reached the large boxes of matches that I would be burned to death! Cousin Lloyd roughs me up a bit on his return home. It seems I had dented his gas tank! Nothing else wrong with the bike. Some lessons are painful.

Near this building Pop-Pop planted his short rows of onion sets in the spring time. Along with lettuce and radish beds. Also tobacco. In the fall Pop-Pop would burn a brush pile and in the spring tobacco seeds were planted and covered in the ashes. No soil. Then small plants were transplanted in rows every 3 feet. Plants would grow to 5 or 6 feet high with huge leaves. In the fall the plants were cut down, hung upside down in the ware room to dry. Later Pop-Pop cut off the leaves, moistened them with his mixture of honey, brown sugar and water, then rolled a leaf into a cigar. The cigars were stored in the summer kitchen to dry. And then Pop-Pop smokes them. On the same lot with the ware room is a garage next to Emerick's home. Pop-Pop's Reo Flying Cloud touring sedan is stored here. I have never seen Pop-Pop drive this car. But this kid must have driven it at least 10,000 miles. The large wooden steering wheel is exactly the right fit for this kid's fingers! It is a 4 door sedan with a canvas top that folds back!

Let's go inside the store. Near the pot belly stove are 2 rocking chairs as well as assorted kegs and boxes, all used by customers and loafers a like. Persons who came in and opened their suitcases of samples were known as drummers. Usually they came from Cumberland but Mr. McFarland, who sold candy, and opened a display case that was a temptation to this kid, lived in Mt. Savage. Pop-Pop's glasses are usually up on his forehead but when he puts on his visor cap and becomes a notary public to prepare a customer's legal papers the glasses are pulled down to where they should be. Pop-Pop has a "Seal of the Commonwealth" which he stamps on every legal paper brought to him. On Saturday evenings, the old timers would gather around the potbelly stove, swap stories, tell jokes, share troubles, argue politics and have a good time till closing time. Sometime my Uncles Ralph & Ray Welsh sing, play the harmonica and guitar while Grandpa Welsh would hop up on the counter top and dance a jig while clapping his hands. That was real fun and could my uncles sing! I think Grandpa Welsh is tetched in the head but I find out that he is just a jovial person. Many loud arguments were about Herb Hoover, whoever he was! At closing, Pop-Pop fixed the fire and together we shuttered the doors and the windows next to the railroad tracks, locked the doors and go into the room. A piece of pie, a drink and we're off to bed. Sometimes, after Mom-Mom dies, I sleep with Pop-Pop-not always! Pop-Pop always kneels at the bed and prays to God the Father. I never prayed. I went to sleep.

Once, I stole a box of White Owl Cigars out of Pop-Pop's store and denied it when Pop-Pop asked me afterwards! The only time this kid ever lied to Pop-Pop. I never understand why Pop-Pop grows his own cigars when he has at least 10 or more boxes in his tobacco showcase-all brands!

On Pop-Pop's lot across the road from Joe Emerick's house are two sloping doors under which is a pair of steps, another door and inside, in the winter time, we find cabbage, apples, pears, carrots, turnips and parsnips buried in boxes of soil with just their tops protruding. Bushels of potatoes. This Is a cave or sometimes called a fruit cellar. On the hill, behind the cave, stands a "July Sweet" apple tree-bushels of apples in early summer. Anyone in Cooks Mills is free to help themselves as long as they last. The field of alfalfa is harvested by a neighbor for bunny and cattle food. On the back side of the property, next to Emericks, stands an old, tall "Northern Spy"- delicious apples in the fall, if one is lucky enough to knock one down with a rock or a piece of wood thrown skyward! The trick is to throw and then catch your prize and not get hit by whatever you threw up! Every delicious "Northern Spy" had its very unusual marking like a healed cut. In the side yard, near the coal pile are 2 very large pear trees. They are loaded every year with large pears, absolutely worthless! Stepping out of the kitchen and along the board walk we find sour cherry trees, a woodshed, plum and prunes, a small chicken coop where we find the banty eggs, a grape arbor, and at the end of the boardwalk a two-seater with the usual Montgomery catalog. Also in the back yard there are several elderberry bushes, some currants, some clumps of rhubarb, and a little horse-radish. In a small plot here in the backyard Pop-Pop grows tomatoes, peas, beans, corn, squash and eggplant. In late summer Pop-Pop dries peaches, plums, prunes and apples. The sliced fruit is put on trays set up on the metal woodshed roof, covered with netting to keep insects off and dried by the sun. In the winter, that fruit is good eating, on cereal, in pies, cooked or uncooked. Pop-Pop's favorite was prunes so it seems, we have cooked prunes day in and day out! In late summer Pop-Pop picks some large choice tomatoes, puts their seeds on a sheet of newspaper, sets it in the sun and when the seeds are dry he scrapes them off the paper with his pocket knife, puts them in a large envelope and waits for spring to arrive so he can plant them! Marglobe and Rutgers are his favorites!

Summer Sunday afternoons we walk up the B & 0 railroad tracks about 1 1/2 miles and back home or we often crossed over to the Pennsylvania railroad tracks along Wills Mountain to the Lang house (long abandoned) then on to the Kinton house and returned home. It is pure delight to walk with Pop-Pop. He knows everything and this kid has lots of "whys", "what's" or 'how's". Many times we drink from the "Lang" spring or the "Kinton" spring- delicious water! Late spring we hunt mushrooms after Sunday School. Summertime we pick dewberries. Then black raspberries and later blackberries. All growing in the wild. All used for jams, jellies, pies or cobblers. In very late summer we trek up on Wills Mountain to pick huckleberries, sometimes near the top of the mountain and often at "Slip Rock" near the bottom. Huckleberries make very delicious pies and cobblers. On Wills Mountain we have to be very careful for there are poisonous rattlesnakes any place we pick berries! We were never bitten. What good times we have together on the mountain. Pop-Pop packs our lunch in a basket. We drink from the spring on top of Wills Mountain and then try to fill the basket with berries before starting down the long abandoned bark road., so named because years before the road was used by horses and wagons to haul bark to the tannery at Hyndman. Dad told me he drove a team as a young person after putting a sprag (a pole) between the two rear wheels and sliding the two rear wheels downgrade to the foot of the mountain. The sprag was the only brake for the trip down! About 1 mile from top to bottom, and several curves.

What good times Pop-Pop and I share together! But storm clouds are on the horizon. Hard times are coming. Older folks say, "The Depression is here." A man comes and tacks up a notice on the front of Pop-Pop's store. Sheriff Sale. What's that? The man puts a chain through the door handle and padlocks the chain together! We can't go in or out! The year is 1930. There is a sale. Pop-Pop and I have to move out! For several days we carry clothing, shoes and what have you down across the railroad tracks to our new home. We made several trips using Pop-Pop's wooden wheelbarrow. The largest thing we took was Pop-Pop's chest, a large wash bowl with the matching pitcher, shaving mug, straight razor,

razor strap, the Good Book, a derby hat, long john underclothes and lots of letters and papers on the tray in the top of his trunk. It is hard to leave such a friendly familiar place but, "Pop-Pop you go on ahead, I want to say goodbye to my gnarled, half rotten good friend, the Northern Spy that gives me such good eating every fall. Good-bye Spy-now you belong to another person." In going across the railroad tracks to that 2 story tan home with green trim around doors and windows, to my home, my birthplace, I've done it, I've traveled down memory lane-back home again! We find Mom, Jane, Bob, Junior, Betty age 5, Leslie age 2 and baby Marilyn age 1. Dad is still at work-won't be home till about 6:30-just in time for supper. What a change this is from 2 of us at Pop-Pop's to 10 of us here now. My family are not strangers to me since I did visit them quite a few times during the 2 years they lived at 419 Grand Ave. Cumberland, Maryland. For 10 cents I could board the Accommodation train at noon, ride to the railroad station in Cumberland, walk to South Cumberland, visit on Saturday, go to the Virginia Ave. movies and then return to Cooks Mills Sunday evening on the train. The Hap Peters lived in half the house at 419 and the Grimms lived next door. They were good friends of the Stallings family.

Getting back to my birthplace I remember one thing that happens here before I went to live at the store with Mom-Mom and Pop-Pop. I'm barefoot in the backyard. It's hot. I see Mother through the open kitchen door. She is doing something in the kitchen, near the table. Then she comes out, crosses the porch, down the steps onto the boardwalk carrying something. At the end of the boardwalk she steps up into the summer kitchen, puts something on the table and us kids all share food with Mother. Mother wore a dark blue middie blouse with a large collar down the back with a large white star in each lower corner. Mother was sweating and wisps of hair fell down over her forehead and eyes.

Mother disappears from my memory and now she is "up on the hill". Our somewhat triangular home place is surrounded by the railroad tracks on one side, by the mill race on another side, and by the public road on the other side. A large garden separates our homes from the railroad. Walking down the road, at the corner of our property a painted wooden picket fence with hops growing on it extends in two directions. In the front yard near the large bay window stand 2 tall cedar trees. In the side yard we see the familiar camperdown elm with its umbrella like shape. This is my birthplace! The Stallings home. Alongside the home is a large smoke house, two summer kitchens at the rear of our home, a wood and coal shed and a two-seater at the end of the dirt path. Two clotheslines between the woodshed and the two-seater which is surrounded by large lilac bushes. In our backyard are plum, peach and sour cherry trees. Out in the orchard stands a partly burned pound apple tree. It was too close to our barn which burned down. I remember all the excitement as I watched it burn from the upstairs window of Pop-Pop's bedroom. Fire to the sky. Near the pound apple, unburned, is the Maiden Blush-good for eating and good for cooking applesauce or dumplings. The Maiden Blush gives us bushels of good apples every year! Close by is the huge "SheepNose"-good eating! About ten trees in our orchard aren't worth much at all. In the far end of our lower yard, near the neighbor's huge storage shed is our barn which Dad built with some help. It is home for a cow and a "tin Lizzie". Over near the mill race stands the pig pen which Dad also built and here two or three pigs are usually kept for butchering in the fall. Outside the kitchen, near the smokehouse, is our well with the familiar pitcher pump while nearby we have an underground cistern. Rainwater off the roof of our home is diverted into the Cistern for all uses except drinking!

Now, let's go inside our new home by way of the front door. We walk up the steps across a small porch into the hallway. On the left is the front room (living room) with the bay window, on the right is the parlor reserved for special company-seldom used! A stairway leads us to the spare bedroom on the left and to Pop-Pop's large bedroom on the right. From our front entrance we can also go down a hall alongside the stairs and exit out on the rear porch. From the rear porch we can enter either the dining room or the kitchen. From the kitchen we go up the stairs to the second floor. Dad and Mom's bedroom on the left and from the hallway into the girls' bedroom and through the girls' bedroom into the boys' bedroom and from our bedroom into Pop-Pop's. This is our home! From our kitchen we go into the dining room and on into the living room with its huge lion's paw library table. In the kitchen a floor to ceiling cupboard opened on either the kitchen side or the dining room side-really convenient! On top of this cupboard Dad keeps his revolver and the bottles of mercury. Sometimes Dad keeps his revolver under his mattress! In the kitchen is the coal-wood cook stove with its huge water tank on the side. A heating oven up on the top. In the living room we have a Heatrola until Dad installs a furnace.

Sometime after Mother dies, Dad marries Emma Rae Landis. Now she's "Mom" to seven lively kids! Until this time, Pop-Pop always told me what to do, when to do it and usually how to do it, but now a new voice comes into my life! Mom tells me to do something. I disagree and when she tries to catch me I run out the path across the millrace out to the island alongside Wills creek where I'm safe, she can't catch me! The story does not end here. This evening after supper dishes are washed Mom tells Dad what happened today and would you believe it? Dad pulls off his belt fast as lightning and applies it to my rear. After quite a few lessons I learn! Mom can tell me what to do! Jane and I wash and dry the supper dishes. After some squabbling we decided to take turns. She wash-I dry. I wash-she dry! Bob and I must fill the wood box, the coal box, the kindling box and the water tank on the side of our cook stove. The 40 gallon iron kettle near the wood shed must be filled on Sunday evening. Carrying the water from beyond the millrace from Wills Creek. The stove tank also must receive water (soft water) from Wills Creek! Our well water was "hard" having limestone in the water-good drinking but not good for washing clothes or dishes. Bob and I used 5 gallon buckets, not filling them too full for the long trips needed to fill kettle and tank. After supper the kitchen table is cleared and we kids get to our school work-no ifs ands or buts! Pop-Pop loves us kids but soon the three little ones, Betty, Leslie and Marilyn become the apple of his eye, and they get most of his attention! When Betty starts to school Mom spends a long time making her curls. Mom says Betty looks just like Shirley Temple. School days with evening chores, both at home and at Mrs. Shoemakers and Mrs. Wills, did not leave much time for playing but we might get in some hide and seek or a game of Old Maid. Saturdays, we boys would roll our hoops, play "Shinny", go fishing or swimming or boating on Will's Creek eddy. Shinny is hockey played with an empty evaporated milk can. We pick sides, draw lines on the road about 50 paces apart, pick a spot in the middle to place the can, count 1-2-3 and both sides make a dash to get the can first and then try to get it across the other teams goal and score a point. 10 points and we have a winner. We usually played with Merle and Frank Mason, James and John Phillips (twins) Jim and Bill Scritchfield and us Stallings kids. We made our own hockey sticks and when playing no hands could ever touch the milk can. We needed lots of cans for when a game ended the milk can was usually a thin, battered piece of tin. Nothing serious until Frank Mason got hit in the leg and got blood poisoning-almost lost his leg! That was the end of our Shinny games. Pop-Pop often made us "Mumblety Pegs" and we play it a lot. We play marbles, cowboys and Indians. We make our own bows and arrows. A nice hickory branch, a strong piece of cord and a straight shaft. Pop-Pop makes our ball bats also he takes a straight piece of sumac about 15 inches long, heats a poker red hot, makes a hole through the sumac. Next he makes a plunger out of wood to fit the hole. We chew newspaper or magazines to get a wad of paper. Plug it in one end of the blow gun, chew another wad, get it good and wet, then blow air in the open end of the gun, and quickly push in the second wad, insert the plunger, look for a good target like the back of someone's head! Push the plunger and hope it was aimed straight and if it was-get ready to run because that usually irritated the person who was hit!

We spend lots of time in Wills Creek because when the mill race was running full it was too dangerous and when it wasn't running we had only dirty holes with trapped small fish and minnows. We spend much time together playing under the camperdown elm tree. We make baskets with the burdock burrs we pick in our back yard. We swing under the camperdown elm. Sometimes we picnic under the elm-our favorite spot to play.

The girls play with their dolls. Lloyd brought big dolls and little dolls home from Lancaster for the girls. Pop-Pop often mysteriously comes up with suckers, or pink and white lozenges for the little ones! The little ones shared slices of Pop-Pop's apple while we bigger kids have to get our own. Sometimes we older kids fight to get whatever Dad might have left in his lunch bucket on his return home. When Dad brings the Saturday Evening Post Jane and I always try to be first to read it! I just can't wait to see how Tugboat Annie makes out in her running feud with that old bully Cap'n Hornblow! What a great story that is! Tugboat Annie usually out smarts that old skipper! And I'm glad, but it is never easy for her to win the battle.

Things are not always peaches and cream here at my new home. Sometimes when Mom antagonizes me too much I purposely disobey her and then run off to our club house on the island. High water had left some boards, we borrowed some from Dad and with borrowed burlap and tar paper we build our club house hangout. This is a safe place until supper time. Dad comes home and he promptly and efficiently applies justice to my back side. Seems like some kids just never learn! I never ran from Dad-never once even gave it a thought!' Mom always has plenty of good food for us kids, fresh baked bread every Thursday with fried dough for supper. Chili con carne is a favorite meal. Spaghetti and meatballs, beans, macaroni and cheese, potatoes, red bread was one of Dad's favorites. We have our own pork, beef, eggs and milk. Lots of milk, cocoa, puddings, cakes. Mom loves parsnips. Yuk! Turnips are OK rutabaga cooked is OK too. Mom skims cream off the top of gallons of milk and churns our own butter-good except early in the spring if our cows found some garlic! Yuk, Yuk! Garlic butter is for the birds! We Stallings' eat good, that's for sure! Sometimes behind the cook stove, there is a 5 gallon crock of root beer in the making, also a 5 gallon crock of "near beer". After the mixes "worked" for a week or so, it was bottled in 1 quart bottles to age for what seems like a lifetime, actually about 2 weeks! Then Mom and we kids enjoy the root beer. Dad alone enjoys the near beer and we kids are never allowed to even taste it. Occasionally, we would hear a loud explosion in the basement and that was one bottle that we never get to drink! Supper ended, dishes done, school work finished, it's off to bed-Junior, Bob and I share the same bed-along with some unwanted, uninvited little creatures! Mom brushes the bed springs with kerosene every spring, sprays the room and gets rid of the little creatures for a time. Each of us boys have a problem, so every spring we go to the Clarks to get new straw and chaff to fill our bed ticks.

We always have warm, neat clothing. Mom sees to that! This year we boys all wear a "Lindy" helmet with goggles. I have flown across the Atlantic at least three or four times without ever leaving the ground! How wonderful! Barb wire fence along the road to school often causes Mom to get out her needle and thread to make repairs! Muddy roads and mud puddles were a pitfall to any ordinary kid and extra work for Mom on wash day!

Dad put together a 16" circular saw on a steel table, a flat pulley, a flat belt, a jacked up rear wheel on the Model T. The belt ran over the pulley and over the rear tire and Dad cuts cross ties into firewood. Pop-Pop cuts firewood with a one man cross cut saw or a bucksaw. Both Dad and Pop-Pop are hard workers.

Life is interesting here, what with cars and trucks going past our home to the Mill and power station. We kids run and jump up on our barn gate and wave at the persons going by. Most drivers wave at us as we wave and holler. One man drove past us kids, turned around at the Mill, and drove past again without even a glance at us hollering and waving kids, up the road and into a passing freight train! He hit the train about 16 cars back of the engine, was dragged up the tracks and finally dumped over the bank into our garden! He was not badly hurt! Mr. & Mrs. Brant rented rooms in our home. He and she in their Dodge truck were hit by the speeding "22", killed instantly. The car was carried almost to the # 8 bridge at the end of our property.

Today I start high school. We cannot ride the school bus so I walk to Stringtown and ride Albright's bus or thumb a ride. Mr. Bert Raley on his way home from working night shift at the Kelly tire plant, picked me up hundreds of times the four years I go to Hyndman High. I am the only boy wearing knickers. The other boys all wore long trousers so I took a lot of kidding. After school we must either ride the Albright bus at $1.50 per week or we can hitchhike along the highway which we do quite often. There were not many cars on the highway but then there were very few who ever passed up a kid hitchhiking! School days were busy days. Deliver the Cumberland Daily News in the morning before school, deliver the Cumberland Evening Times after school, usually around 40 customers, plus the Grit twice a month on Saturday plus the usual chores-fill the wood box, fill the coal box, fill the water tank on the side of our cook stove, do homework, play and eat. Our Dad can do anything, he cuts glass to repair the windows our balls break, he gardens after work, even builds a wire cage so that lima beans can be picked from the underside of the cage. He drew up a blueprint of our home, sent the print to Montgomery Ward and they sent us a coal burning furnace with all pipes, registers and elbows made to order. Dad installed the whole works in our home replacing the Heatrola. We even had upstairs registers! Dad burned sugar, Mom added milk, cream, sugar and whatever else and we churned a freezer of ice cream. Dad and us bigger kids would walk up the railroad tracks, pick a gallon of teaberries which Dad would mash with a potato masher and then Mom completed the mixture and again we churn a freezer of delicious teaberry ice cream. We boys get the privilege of churning. Many times Lloyd and his friend Mac would show up after the churning was finished. We never did find out how they always showed up after the work was done. But they did!

Once each year Dad brings home several gallons of both white and dark soup. The result of one baby snapper turtle put in a huge barrel, fed lunch box scraps by the thirty-one Potomac Edison River Plant employees for one year and then ending up in the soup pot! Our Dad is a real genius. He moves a small building to the Cooks Mills Dam and on Saturdays and Sundays he sells candy, chewing gum, homemade hot dogs, homemade hamburgers, homemade ice cream and sometimes 5 or 10 gallons of ice cream purchased from Lear and Oliver in Cumberland. Dad usually sold out of everything to the one hundred or more persons gathered there to swim and have family get-togethers. One Sunday afternoon amid all the noise and confusion in the water Dad heard a call for help for the third time. He jumped off a 16 foot cliff, clothes and all and brought a lady safely to shore. He saved her life! When the clutch and ruxtle gear burned out on our Ford in winter Dad removed the parts, brought them in to the kitchen floor, repaired them and put them back in the Ford with no help! When the car is out of order and Albright's bus is not running Dad leaves for work at 3 AM to walk the eleven miles to the River Plant by 7 AM. He walks home too-after a day's work! Dad has one failing. We can look up the road, see Dad one half mile away and know whether or not he had stopped at the "Blue Goose" on a payday! We know his natural walk!

Today I begin my second year of school at Hyndman. Thanks to Mom I wear clean clothes, long trousers, a nice knitted sweater, and leather shoes. I've have a good breakfast-oatmeal, toast, cocoa- must leave early to either get picked up by Mr. Bert Raley or catch Albright's bus, at 15 cents per trip. Sisters Jane and Betty, brothers Bob and Junior will be walking up across the railroad tracks to catch their bus for the trip to Consolidated School beyond Hyndman. Little brother Leslie and baby sister Marilyn will have Mom and Pop-Pop all to themselves today! See you all this evening! Dad will be home about 6:30 from his day at work. Once again its supper time in the Stallings home.

Today is Wed. February 27, 2002

I am so very thankful that a merciful God would enable this old codger to look backwards eighty years and live again the first fifteen years of my life -how gracious Thou art! I praise my Lord Jesus that many faces, many scenes are still brilliantly clear in spite of the long interval of time. Some few have faded a bit! Thank you Lord Jesus for my visit back home. It was truly wonderful. Now I set my face homeward again-toward my eternal home. Awaiting your call to enter through those portals of Glory into the very presence of the One who hung on Calvary's cross in my stead. That will be Glory! I will be home!

Memories of Anna Lee Stair

Mrs. Anna Lee (Clark) Stair was born 90 years ago in the farmhouse where she currently resides. The original farmhouse dates from the late 1700's to early 1800's. Her parents were George and Elenora (Stouffer) Clark. Anna Lee had two brothers: Olin (Pete) and John. She married Gerald Stair, who was from a neighboring farm. She has four children: Sandy, Jerry Lee, Debbie, and Perry Alan. Anna Lee has gratiousy shared some of her life memories and experiences in the following pages.

I recall that we used to ice skate on the frozen creek and sled ride as well. Also we made lots of ice cream when the weather provided us ice to use.

Trains stopped at all the little towns. I used to ride the Pennsylvania RR to Madley, PA to visit with my Grandpa Stouffer. I used to walk over the B & O Bridge to get to the other side of Wills Creek. The Pennsylvania RR ran on the East side of Wills Creek. The B & O Station was at the south side of the crossing.

There were 2 lime kilns in the area. One was south of Cooks Mill the other was up Grange Hall Road. The south of Cooks Mill was located behind the Gorsuch Farm (aka Christmas Tree Farm) and the product was hauled to Cumberland.

Deals was located across the tracks. This is where the power plant was. Potomac Edison eventually bought the power plant and all of its equipment. The Kennel house that is currently there, sits on the foundation of the Cornelius DeVore home.

The Gas Station at the Crossroads, since closed, was constructed on the site of the former school. When schools were consolidated, the children were bused to Hyndman. They would ride the Albright Bus Line with Mr. Carpenter driving the children. This was also the location of a church before the church was constructed at its present location in about 1843.

Mail was received at Cooks Mill via the railroad with the Post Office being operated by Mr. Stallings. Mr. Stallings Post Office was located right across the tracks at the crossing. There was also a mail path up over Wills Mountain in which mail was carried over to Centerville.

I recall that the Osters lived in a house behind Burleys. Not only was there a swinging bridge to cross Wills Creek, but there was also a place where cars could ford the stream to get to the other side.

The Welcome Inn was operated by the Troutmans and Divelbliss'. The Divelbliss' lived just north of the Gorsuch Farm (Christmas Tree Farm). I remember one night we were called from Hyndman one night about cows that were struck and killed on the train tracks near the Gorsuch Farm. We were lucky that they were not ours.

People often recall the little Smouse house on the corner of the Crossroads that was cut in half to make room for the upgraded road as it came through the area.

The ball field was located just across the Gladdens Run Bridge on the right side in Cooks Mill. This was the location of many softball games.

My husband Jerry worked on the railroad. He would send me hand signals as he passed through Cooks Mill and this would let me know if I needed to go pick him up or if he had a ride home to Cooks Mill. It was not uncommon for hobos to pass through the area. Story has it that they had a way of marking houses if they were treated good so that other hobos would know which houses to call on. Often we would feed them. If they needed to stay we would put them up in the barn but only if they did not have any matches.

My husband's hand signals were not the only signals we used in Cooks Mill. Pearl Lowery, Emma Diehl, and I had a system to signal one another when we had errands to run outside of the house. Emma was our driver and the system involved us hanging sheets on the line.

As a teenager, I found employment working at the funeral home in Hyndman answering the phones while the funeral director was out at the cemetery. I never recalled a single call for service coming in while I was manning the phones. I also remember that funerals would leave the Cooks Mill Church and go directly up over the top of the hill to the cemetery. The cemetery road had not yet been constructed.

My husband Jerry grew up in his home place just across and up from where Shroyer's Plumbing is located. His uncle George owned and operated the Blue Spring Dairy and George would go door to door selling his milk. The bread man would also deliver bread door to door. It was Bunny Bread.

As a member of the church, we used to go down to the area between Ford's Mill and Amos See's house for our annual festival. We would have hamburgers and hot dogs as well as ice cream. We used to also do yearly Christmas plays at church.

When the County Fair was coming to town, it was a big day for us. We would go up and watch the fair arrive and set up all day on Sunday as the convoy would come into Bedford. We would go back at least one more day for the fair itself.

Here on the farm we had a spring house with running water. It had two levels in it which allowed us to keep things cool. The water from the spring would flow through into a trough for the animals to drink from near the barn. I recall during the 1936 flood that our barn and garden were flooded.

Above: A 1988 aerial view of the Stair Farm. *Photo courtesy of Anna Lee Stair*

Businesses

Deal Electric Light and Power Plant

Formerly the Cooks Mill Electric Light and Power Company, The Deal Electric Light and Power Company maintained a facility in Cooks Mill. At this location, they placed water driven turbines in the water and controlled their flow utilizing a dam and control gates to regulate the flow. The electricity generated was then piped out to the areas south of Cooks Mill including Ellerslie. Interesting to note was the fact that the electricity initially was only available during the day time. The Deals also operated a grist mill in the same area once again using the water flow to power the milling operation.

The plant itself had a 6 cylinder gasoline engine mounted on heavy timbers. This engine was used to generate the power when the water was low or not flowing. The dam was located upstream. The gate of the dam was constructed with large sycamore timbers due to their ability to remain in the water for long periods of time. The concrete foundations still remain from the turbines. When the plant closed, one turbine could not be removed and it was left behind.

The Deal Bros. maintained offices in Cumberland on Glenn Street in a building that still stands and bears their name. The building was also the location of the mill they maintained in Cumberland. This milling operation was destroyed by a large fire in 1908.

Above: This photo shows the channel under the road that allowed water to divert to the power company turbines. *Photo courtesy of Marilynn Kennell.*

Below: The receipt is from the Deal Electric Light and Power Plant for electricity used by Mr. Sam Kennell. In this case the bill was $1.71 for the month. *Photo courtesy of Marilynn Kennell.*

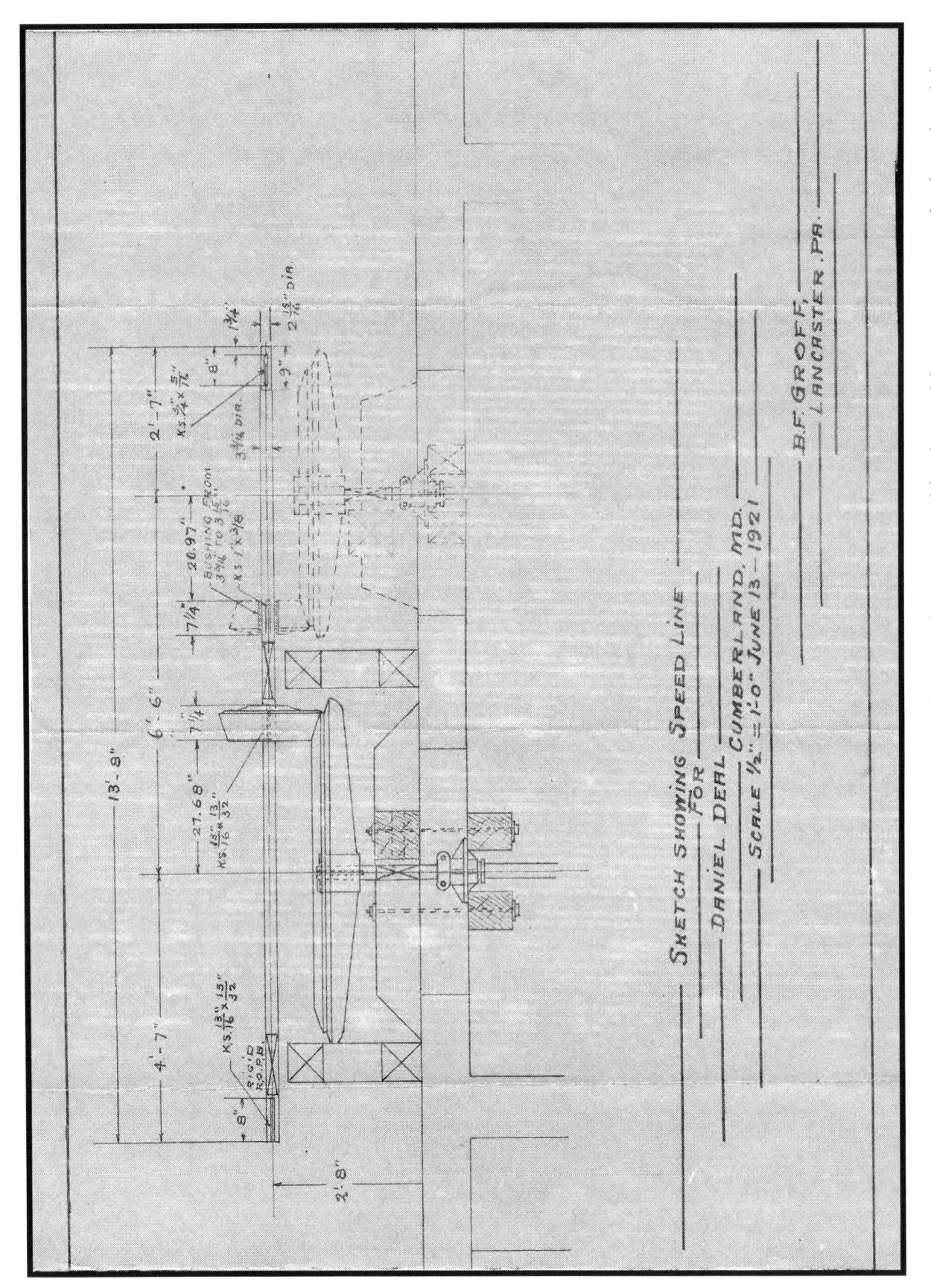

Above: This design drawing represents part of the equipment that was used in the turbines to generate hydro-electricity from the Deal Electric Plant in Cooks Mill. *Photo courtesy of Marilynn Kennell.*

ESTABLISHED 1862

THE JAMES LEFFEL & CO.

MANUFACTURERS OF

TURBINE WATER WHEELS
STEAM ENGINES AND BOILERS

CABLE ADDRESS:
"LEFFEL SPRINGFIELD, OHIO"

LONG DISTANCE BELL TELEPHONE
MAIN 59

ADDRESS ALL COMMUNICATIONS
TO THE COMPANY

B. F. GROFF, EASTERN SALES ENGINEER
OFFICE 556
WOOLWORTH BLDG.

LONG DISTANCE TELEPHONE
BELL 530 X

TELEGRAPH CODES USED:
LEFFEL'S PRIVATE
LIEBER'S STANDARD, WESTERN UNION,
A.B.C. 4TH AND 5TH EDITION CLAUSEN-THUE,
ENGINEERING WITH SUPPLEMENT, BUSINESS,
LIEBERS FIVE LETTER AMERICAN,
A.B.C. 5TH EDITION CLAUSEN-THUE IMPROVED
BENTLEYS COMPLETE PHRASE CODE.

LANCASTER, PA. May 31, 1921.

ALL CONTRACTS AND AGREEMENTS ARE CONTINGENT UPON STRIKES, ACCIDENTS OR OTHER CAUSES BEYOND OUR CONTROL AND SUBJECT TO APPROVAL AT THE HOME OFFICE AT SPRINGFIELD, OHIO.
ALL QUOTATIONS F.O.B. FACTORY, SPRINGFIELD, OHIO, UNLESS OTHERWISE STATED, AND ARE FOR PROMPT ACCEPTANCE ONLY.
ALL RIGHTS RESERVED TO CORRECT ERRORS ON QUOTATIONS, OR ANY OTHER MATTER HEREIN.

Mr. Daniel Deal,
Cooks Mills, Pa.

Dear Sir:-

Under separate cover I am mailing to you drawing showing the proposed arrangement and installation of the 50" Right Hand Upright Standard Samson Turbine. Also pair of bevel mortice gears; 1 Vertical Finished Water Wheel Shaft; 1 Horizontal Finished shaft; also one Vertical Water Wheel shaft bearing. All as specified in contract dated May 11, 1921. Please go over this drawing and if you have any comments to make, please advise me promptly as the order has been entered at the factory for shipment on or about July 15th. Am also furnishing the cast iron bushing for your present cast iron pinion. Will secure a price on the thrust bearing as shown on the drawing and will quote you price later on. I understand that your freight station, B. & O. is a prepaid station. Therefore will prepay the freight and render invoice for freight charges. Presume you are in position to take care of the shipment of the turbine also the gearing, etc. at the B. & O. Station for the reason that there is no freight house at the station and therefore am writing you in regard to receiving the shipment. Please let me hear from you by return mail, and oblige

Yours respectfully,

Above: The above letter is correspondence between Daniel Deal and the James Leffel & Co. for the purchase and installation of the turbine for the Deal Electrical Plant. This letter details the shipment via rail to the Cooks Mill area. *Photo courtesy of Marilynn Kennell.*

Cook's Mill Electric Light and Power Co.

PUBLIC SERVICE COMMISSION OF MARYLAND

ORDER No. 2555.

In the matter of

The Application of the COOK'S MILL ELECTRIC LIGHT AND POWER COMPANY for an Order Permitting and Approving the Transfer of All of Its Property, Rights and Franchises to Daniel Deal.

Before the

Public Service Commission of Maryland.

Case No. 1021.

The matter of the application of the Cook's Mill Electric Light and Power Company, a corporation of Allegany County, Maryland, to cease to do business as such and to transfer all its property and franchises to Daniel Deal, and the supplemental application of Daniel Deal to continue the business hitherto done by the said corporation and to exercise the franchises hitherto exercised by said Cook's Mill Electric Light and Power Company coming on to be heard after due notice published in compliance with the Order of this Commission passed January 7th, 1916, and no protests thereto having been made, and the Commission having determined after hearing that the exercise of the said franchise by said Cook's Mill Electric Light and Power Company, for the special reasons and under the special conditions set forth in the application, is no longer necessary and convenient for the public service, and that the exercise of the franchise heretofore exercised by said corporation by said Daniel Deal is necessary and convenient for the public service,

IT IS, THEREFORE, This 4th day of February, in the year nineteen hundred and sixteen, by the Public Service Commission of Maryland,

ORDERED, (1) That the Cook's Mill Electric Light and Power Company be, and it is hereby, authorized to cease doing business and to transfer all its property, rights and franchises to Daniel Deal.

(2) That the exercise by said Daniel Deal of the franchises heretofore exercised by said Cook's Mill Electric Light and Power Company be, and the same is hereby, permitted and approved.

Two Franchises to Light Ellerslie

Road Directors Grant Competing Companies

Right to Sell Current for 25 Years

The Allegany County Road Directors yesterday granted a franchise each to the Cook's Mills Electric Light and Power Company and the Andrew Ramsey Corporation to light the town of Ellerslie.

The franchises permit the companies to erect poles along the public highway for the purpose of furnishing electric light and power. The Ramsey Corporation has the right to erect poles from a point near Ellerslie to Corriganville, and the other company from the State Line to Corriganville.

The Andrew Ramsey Corporation was represented by De Warren J. Reynolds, attorney who said he secured the passage through the Legislature of an act enabling the said corporation to consolidate its Ellerslie and Mt. Savage plants and that his company had purchased considerable land in and around Ellerslie upon which to erect an immense power and electric Light plant to supply power to its other plants, and incidentally light and power to subscribers. Mr. Reynolds said he could not promise just when his company would be ready to go to work but that it would be in the near future. By the franchise the county in both instances, is to be made harmless and the said companies are to supply the town of Ellerslie with one 32 candle power electric light for every 25 subscribers.

The Cook's Mill Electric and Power plant is erected on the Pennsylvania side of the line at Cook's Mill, and is owned by Deal Brothers of this city. J. W. S. Cochrane, attorney said they had their plant ready for business.

The attorney to the road directors, Walter C. Capper, prepared the agreements, which forbid the assignment of the franchise without the consent of the road directors.

Mr. Reynolds said that under the State law a charge was made of 25 centers for each pole erected and that his company was willing to pay that sum. This, however, was not inserted in the franchise granted. The Andrew Ramsey Corporation was given two years in which to erect its plant. The matter of rates was discussed, but it was decided that was a matter with which the public utilities commission only could deal. The franchises are similar, being for twenty-five years, during which time the county is to be indemnified for any damages or claims.

The Ramsey Corporation offered to pay an annual tax of 25 cents per pole to the town of Ellerslie, the equivalent in electrical current, which would light the streets of the town free.

Date Unknown but approximately 1903

Welcome Inn

WELCOME INN

On Highway Between Cumberland, Md. and Hyndman, Pa.   2460-30

The Welcome Inn was located on the top of Stairs Hill in Palo Alto. The Inn also served as a gas station, as some of the following photographs depict, and had cottages to rent. The inn was owned by Match Albright.. Harry Smouse operated the gas station below in the 1930s.

Above: This is a photography of Florence Divelbliss. Her husband, John and herself owned the Welcome Inn on the top of Stairs Hill. The Welcome Inn can be seen in the background. It is believed that at one time they were a Sinclair gasoline dealer.

The Crossroads Service Station

Above and Below: These two photographs are of the service station constructed by Mr. Harry Smouse. This was also the site of the former school. The service station would eventually be removed and the land used for residential use. It is located in the area known as Stringtown, Pennsylvania.

Right: There were two swinging bridges to cross Will's Creek in Cooks Mill. One was located above the Stair Farm and was used to reach the PA Rail Road Depot. The second, pictured here, was located behind the Gorsuch farm and was used to reach the homes behind it. The home pictured here was the George and Charlotte Burley home. Children were known to play on the bridges and work them back and forth to get the bridges rocking to and fro.

Photo courtesy of Anna Stair

Left: The photograph, shows the old dance hall that was located in the area. The dance hall was located up Stringtown Hollow but was visible from Rt. 96. It was known for its entertainment in the area. Saturday nights were dance night with bands brought in for the music.

Photo courtesy of Marilynn Kennell

Henry W. Ford's Grist Mill

Not far from Cooks Mills is the old Ford's Mill that has existed for decades. Located off PA Rt. 96, the red wood structure is at the intersection with Landis Road. The mill was constructed and operated By Henry W. Ford and was later transferred to his son Frank Ford. Frank resided in the white house adjacent to the mill. The sole purpose of the mill was to take whole grains and grind them into usable flours. Some of these grains, notably the buckwheat and wheat flour, would actually be marketed under the mill's own label for sale. The grains could be wheat, corn, or even buckwheat. The buckwheat required the most time to grind and only one grain could be ground at a time. The mill also sold straw and hay in addition to the ground flours.

Often farmers would bring their wagons to the mill. These would be loaded down with grains to be ground. The farmers would wait for their product often bringing lunch for themselves as well as feed for their team of horses. Customers of the mill would come from Kennell's Mill, Corriganville and even Bard and Tiger Valley. Rarely, for some reason, would they have customers from Cooks Mills.

The mill had a rather large delivery area that included Mt. Savage to West of Mann's Choice to an area known as Smoke Corner. Edgar Stallings then just a teenager worked with the Fords making deliveries in a 1936 Dodge truck. Mr. Stallings quipped during this interview that he did not even possess a driver's licenses at the time. Orders were placed in advance and Mr. Stallings would deliver. Many times lines of credit were provided but on some deliveries into Mt. Savage he remarked about always coming home with $2 dollar bills. If a customer would bring grain to the mill to have it ground, the customary practice was to take 1/7 of the final product as payment. Mr. Stallings worked at the mill for about two years would ride his bike to work from his home in Cooks Mill.

The mill operations were powered by water, with a backup straight 8 cylinder gasoline engine. The mill would operate chillingly quiet under water power, but if water was not available for example as the result of a rare freezing over, the gasoline motor would be called into service. This motor sometimes had to be warmed by a small fire underneath to get it to start. Once the motor was engaged, the whole mill would shake as the motor was mounted on timbers 20 inches high by 12 inches wide. The water would pass through a concrete slues located below a dam located across form the Logsdon Farm. This dam would be controlled to control the flow of water through the mill. The water for the operation would travel down and pass under Rt. 96. It was this water that powered the mill utilizing an undershot wheel, meaning this wheel powered the mill by rotating downward. This would power the mill stones and allow them to begin the process of grinding. Envision if you will two stones about four feet in diameter, with the bottom stone holding a fixed position and the top stone rotating to grind. This top stone would have grooves in it to accommodate the whole grains being drawn through. The ground grain would then be carried by a series of buckets on a conveyor and would be dumped on sifting screens to sort out size. The flour would be shifted through a silk cloth. The size of the grind was actually controlled by adjusting the gap between the two stones. Just the thought of making such precision adjustments on heavy stones is mind boggling. If the gap was too fine the flour would burn, or if the gap was too large, the grind would be to course. The mill was basically a two man operation. Once it started, it really on required one man to feed the grinder.

The mill would remain in operation to winter time opening at 8 AM and closing around 5 PM. A couple of weeks each year would be carved out to use a hammer and chisel to sharpen the top mill stone. An all wood mill, the operators would use wooden tools to raise the stone to a vertical position to do this sharpening work.

The mill had a basement in it. It was in that basement that often apples would be collected from an island in the stream. These bushels of apples would be stored over winter in the basement. The mill basement had 10 foot ceilings. The mill also had an attic area that was used for storage and it was nothing to run a 90 lb. bag of flour up the steps to store. The Hyndman side of the building housed an office and stove. Mr. Stallings recalled one winter day when the temperature was 30 degrees below zero. He fired the stove up but was provided refuge in the Charlie Landis house until the mill warmed up. The home actually housed two living quarters at one time.

Stallings General Store

The L. I. Stallings General Merchandise Store began in 1878 under the ownership of John H. Stallings. Mr. Stallings operated the store and also served as the postmaster for the community until 1883 when he sold the store and stock to his son Irving. Irving had been employed as the store during the last five years as a clerk. The store occupied the structure pictured above, utilizing a first floor room measuring 40 x 18 feet. The store sold staple groceries, dry goods, hardware, fertilizer and agricultural implements. The store closed in approximately 1929.

Burglar Shoots As Discovered. Two Are Hurt.

Awakened by a burglar, who held a riffle to his face and threatened to shoot, L.I. Stallings, aged 54 years, sa store keeper of Cook's Mills, PA., a short distance from this city, together with his son, Carleton, aged 20 years; his wife, Mrs. Sarah Elizabeth Stallings, and a daughter, Mrs. James Hartsock, of 24 Columbia Avenue, this city, early today had an experience that they will not soon forget. Carleton Stallings, the son, who went to the aid of the father, was shot through the left ear and had his left hand badly slashed by a knife. The burglar got away with little booty.

It was just about 3 o'clock this morning when Stallings was awakened with a command to get up and hand over his cash. He jumped from his bed an grappled with the intruder, at the same time calling his son, who was asleep in the next room. The young man rushed to aid his father and as he did so the burglar shoved the rifle against the side of his ear, inflicting a wound not considered serious.

Mr. Stallings and his son managed to get hold of the burglar but he was a large man and they were unable to hold him, as he used a knife with much effect. Mt. Stallings was cut in the face, receiving a wound on the left check not thought serious. The boy was cut several times on the hand.

Previous to having awakened Mr. Stallings, the thief had entered the room of Mrs. Hartsock and when he discovered it was a woman, Mrs. Hartsock having awakened, he commanded her to keep quiet. She let out a cry of "Burglars" which awakened Mrs. Stallings and the man ran to her pushing the gun in her face and threatening to murder her if she made an outcry. Mr. Stallings awakened at this time.

Incensed by the attack upon the Stallings, Residents in and near Cooks' Mills formed a posse and are scouring the nearby hills for him. Bloodhounds have been sent for and if the man is caught it is feared he will be roughly handled.

Young Stallings came to this city this morning and had his injuries dressed by Dr. A. Leo Franklin. The physician does not believe any of the wounds serious.

The young man in telling of the affair to a reporter of the Cumberland Press today, said that if was an experience he will not soon forget. He said he did his best to capture the burglar , but the man was too much for him. He says that the gun, with which he was shot, was stolen from the store which is on the first floor of the building. Only a few razors and some other small articles were taken. The burglar probably had these in his pockets before he entered the sleeping quarters of the family.

February 23, 1914 Cumberland Evening Times

Discovery of Plaster of Paris

The article appearing below talks about the discovery of Plaster of Paris in the Wills Creek Valley 13 miles above Cumberland. This article appeared in the *Weekly Register*, Volume 49 dated 1835-1836. This talks about how, through the use of the C & O Canal when it was completed, this new product will revolutionize the world. This discovery was made on the land owned by Campbell Henderson and others along Wills Creek. The new discovery will be ground at the mill of Cornelius DeVore for further testing and experiment. It discussed the plans to erect a mill for the gypsum and move forward in a grand scale with this discover.

Cumberland, Maryland, has long been celebrated for the beauty and abundance of its excellent coal—now about to come into "the market" by the Chesapeake and Ohio canal. It is very rich—and high expectations are entertained of it—that will be more than realized. But the "Civilian" of the 10th inst. has the following account of a new discovery that promises also to be of mighty importance to this mountain region of our state.

We have just been informed that an extensive quantity of gypsum, or *plaster of Paris*, has been discovered on the lands owned by Campbell Henderson and others, on Wills' creek, thirteen miles above Cumberland. Mr. H. had some of this plaster ground a year or two ago, and put on clover, and it proved quite equal to the best imported plaster in its effect. It has also been tried in various other ways, with such beneficial effect, as to render it certain of being of a superior quality. Several tons of it, we are further informed, will be ground at Mr. Cornelius Devore's mill, this winter, for further experiment. Mr. H. and others are now making preparations to work the plaster on an extensive scale. Having purchased an eligible site, they purpose the erection of a mill, &c. and there can be no doubt but their investment will prove highly valuable and profitable.

This discovery adds another to the many advantages this section of country possesses in articles of trade, which will be rendered doubly valuable when our different works of internal improvement are completed, and avenues to the different markets are opened, of which our Chesapeake and Ohio canal will afford one of the most important means of transportation.

Railroads

The Railroads Through Cook's Mill

The Pennsylvania Railroad— In 1872, the Pennsylvania Railroad built a line running from Mt. Dallas to the State Line. The purpose was to be able to connect with the Cumberland and Pennsylvania Railroad and enable the PRR stock to reach Cumberland. The PPR would maintain a roundhouse at the Stateline. The Pennsylvania Railroad would pass through Cooks Mill on the east side of Wills Creek. It necessitated a swinging bridge to be able to reach the small station that was located there. Supplies would be off loaded and then moved across the bridge. This railroad was often referred to as the Pennsy by the locals.

The B & O Railroad—The B & O railroad would pass through Cooks Mills on the west side of Wills Creek. Initially it was only one track passing through and a siding was added for the Stalling General Store. Eventually it would become two sets of tracks passing through the community.

The Gladdens Valley Railroad—It was incorporated on July 23, 1903. It began at the Cooks Mills Station on the B & O Railroad and proceeded for 5 miles into Gladdens (Kennels Mill) in Somerset County, Pennsylvania.

Harper, Deal and W. Railroad – It was built about 4 miles in 1912 from Cook's Mills up Gladdens Run to Kennells Mill., Somerset County. It was used to take out lumber. It is unknown what the W. stood for. It was sold in 1915 to Cooks Mills Coal and Clay Company.

Cooks Mills Coal and Clay Co. Railroad—In 1915 the company acquired property of Harper, Deal and W. . From 1912 through 1915 it was used to haul lumber and from 1915 to 1920 it was used to haul coal. Operations then discontinued but the track (dinky track) was not removed until about 1931. It had two small locomotives (donkey engines) which were probably 0-4-OT. The donkey engines stopped at the tipple and the loaded cars were transported across a wooden trestle and dumped inot the waiting railroad cars.

Cooks Mills B & O Train Station

Below: The Cooks Mills Train Station was located near the current crossing. These two photos depict the train station at different perspectives. The first photo shows the train station heading south toward Ellerslie. The second photo shows the train station heading north toward Hyndman, PA. The Stalling family home can be seen in the background. This home burnt to the ground in the early 1940s.

Photos courtesy of Marilynn Kennell

Right: The single rail line of the B&O Railroad included a siding as seen here. This siding was utilized by the Stallings General Store.

Left: The current signal box for CSX at the Cooks Mills Crossing.

Below: A steam train making its way up the B & O tracks near the Stair Farm in Cooks Mills.

Photo courtesy of Anna Stair.

This train accident occurred in occurred in March of 1948 on the B & O Railroad between Ellerslie and Cooks Mill. There were no significant injuries as result of this crash. The east bound freight trail derailed tossing cars onto the west bound freight train.

Photos courtesy of Tim Wilson

Above: This photo was taken around 1950 or 1951. It shows a train accident on the Hyndman side above the Cooks Mill Bridge above the Emma Deal property.

Photo courtesy of Don and Myrna Lowery

The bridge above was located on the west side of Cooks Mill over Will's Creek. This was a four span truss bridge pictured in 1890. Notice that part of the bridge was built over land. This was common with many bridges as fill was not available. This structure was replaced by a plate girder bridge in 1917 with the approach filled in. This bridge was constructed by the King Bridge Company.

Photos courtesy of Marilynn Kennell

Churches

Cooks Mill United Methodist Church

The original Cooks Mill Church can be dated to 1803. Services were held in a log cabin church that was constructed for all denominations. Originally known as DeVore's Meeting House was located along Gladdens Run. It took it's original name from Cornelius DeVore, who was a prominent citizen in the area at the time. The story told indicates that watchmen were placed at the doors during service to look out for the Indians that were in the area. The original church was destroyed by fire in the early 1840s.

In 1843, The Chapel at Cooks Mill, the present church, was constructed. 1n 1862, the 1 3/4 acrea lot was officially purchased from Samuel DeVore by the church for $25.00. In 1963 additional acreage was also donated to the church by Ella Clark.

The trustees fo the Church in 1843 were Henry Cook, John Wilhelm, Jr., Hanson Cook, Benjamin F. Buchanan, William Cook, John Cook, and Benjamin Lowery.

The church is the location of the burial site of Cornelius Devore and his wife Elizabeth. The original Graves were up the hill behind the church. Memorial markers are located down near the church.

Above: The congregation of the Wills Creek Methodist Chapel.

Photo courtesy of Marilynn Kennell

HISTORIC GATHERING

MAY 26, 1984

COOK'S MILLS UNITED METHODIST CHURCH

Two hundred years ago, on Christmas Eve, 60 circuit riding preachers gathered in Baltimore to organize the Methodist Episcopal (ME) Church. More than 40 denominations in the United States today trace their beginnings to that now famous conference.

In tribute to Methodism's 200th year we have assembled a summary of some of the historical events and people that have kept our community and church alive for the past 200 years.

All of the names and dates in this booklet are approximated. The information was gained through many different sources and is accurate to the best of our knowledge.

In researching this project it was found that information was unavailable and very hard to obtain at this date. It is our sincere wish that from this date forward accurate records will be logged to insure availibility to those who may desire to do research at a later date.

Cook's Mills first church was called DeVore's Meeting House. It was located along Gladdens Run. A Methodist preaching circuit-rider, Robert Ayers, served this circuit from 1787-1788. He kept a daily journal which is now in the Lovely Lane Museum in Baltimore. In his journal he mentions Oldtown and coming to Fort Cumberland and coming up Will's Creek to preach at Cornelius DeVore's Meeting House. An article in the Hyndman Bulletin read:

> Cook's Mills-1803
> "Services are being held in the log church constructed for all denominations. We are proud that we have the honor of building the first church in Londonderry Township. It is expected that the building will also be used as a school."

Another article boasted of a new grist mill:

> Cook's Mills-1800
> "The new grist mill built by Cornelius DeVore Sr., first settler, is a daisy. Feed can be ground quickly in this modern mill turned by Will's Creek water. South Londonderry Township is lucky to have such a mill."

The grist mill also housed an electric power plant which supplied electricity for Cook's Mills and Ellerslie. There also was a General Store, a Post Office and a Train Station in Cook's Mills.

In 1820 Michael Porter taught a select school in Cook's Mills. He had no classification except in reading. Cornelius DeVore was one of the first teachers. Benjamin L. Dodge, Edward J. Cotter and R. L. Jones taught at different times. There were then two schools in the township.

In 1843 the Chapel at Cook's Mills, our present church, was constructed after DeVore's Meeting House was destroyed by fire. In 1862 the 1 3/4 acre lot was officially purchased from Samuel DeVore by the church for $25.00. The Trustees of the Church at this time (1843) were: Henry Cook   William Cook
                                John Wilhelm, Jr. John Cook
                                Hanson Cook   Benjamin Lowrey
                                Benjamin F. Buchanan

(In 1963 additional acreage was also donated to the church by Ella Clark.)

In 1877 Mr. David Cook of Will's Creek Chapel assisted Rev. S. S. Wilson, pastor of the Hyndman Circuit, in the organization of a society (church).

An ancient cemetary once occupied the hill behind the Chapel. The names of it's occupants are unknown. The two grave markers at the edge of the church parking lot were placed there in memory of the historic cemetary.

The first rivival meeting at Cook's Mills was held on August 20, 1853 by W. B. Gregg. The second revival meeting commenced on Dec. 31, 1860 and closed Jan. 4th, 1861. The pastor, D. S. Poling, wrote:

> "We had a very interesting meeting. The people of God were considerably revived, and the sinners were at the alter, seeking religion, and one professed to have found peace."

Will's Creek Chapel is located near the base of Will's Mountain. Will's Mountain and Will's Creek are both named for a notorious Indian Chief named Chief Wills. Consequently, the settlers and the Indians must have had some contact with each other. One story that was handed down seems to indicate that during church services someone would always stand guard outside the church in case of a surprise visit!

The Civil War, which started in 1861, had a direct effect on the Methodist Church. Just a few years earlier the ME Church North and the ME Church South went their separate ways due to strong convictions on both sides regarding slavery. After years of negotiations, three major branches of Methodism- the ME Churches North and South and the Methodist Protestants, who had withdrawn from the ME Chruch in 1830- met in 1939 and formed the Methodist Church.

Local research revealed that Ruth Shaffer's grandpap Buchanan was class leader. He lived in Hyndman where Shirley & Glenn Thompson live now. He rode his horse down to the Chapel every 2 weeks to preach. W. C. Brian preached on the Sunday the class leader didn't. That was about 1888. Buchanan was class leader for 22 years.

Around 1950 the basement was dug out to add Sunday School rooms. About 10 years later the front addition was added along with a steeple and bell. The first carpeting was laid in 1959. More recently, red carpet and matching seat cushions, made by the ladies of the church, were added. The beautiful stained glass windows were purchased in 1957. Our latest improvement has been exterior siding and red trim door.

Aside from Sunday School and Church on Sunday and Prayer Meeting on Tuesday evening the church serves many other functions such as:
Ice Cream Socials	Weddings	Showers
Aerobics Classes	Banquets	Covered Dish Dinners
Bible School	UMW Meetings	Birthday Parties

The current officers of the church are: Superintendent-Merle Berkheimer, Secretary-Anna Lee Stair, Treasurer-Donald Messenger, Trustees-Merle Berkheimer, Donald Messenger, Gerald Shroyer, Ed Shaffer and Let Cutler

WEDDINGS HELD AT COOK'S MILLS CHURCH

09-14-46	Kenneth & Delores (Hosselrode) Lowery
06-16-56	Carlton & Patty (Divelbiss) Stair
08-31-57	Jim & Glenna (Rizer) Leydig
03-13-64	Norman & Cheryl (Conners) Sills
05-23-76	Herb & Liz (Wagner) Simmons
11-24-77	Gary & Cindy (Berkheimer) Leap
08-30-80	Todd & Susan (Berkheimer) May
10- -82	Michael & Kelly Jo (Pearcey) Ranker
03-18-83	Brent & Gail (McCoy) Turner
04-18-84	Gary & Kathy (Bridges) Christner

MINISTERS WHO SERVED COOK'S MILLS

1900 - Rev. Benson	1948 - C. F. Crowe
1903 - W. C. Brian	1950 - C. J. Moore
1915 - R. H. Bartlett	1952 - T. E. Richardson
1920 - M. A. Parker	1956 - Paul R. O'Brien
1922 - Charles Lanham	1960 - B. F. Hartman
1924 - W. W. Costeen	1962 - R. C. Chambers
1926 - W. A. Keese	1966 - M. W. Benny, Jr.
1930 - E. A. Godsay	1969 - H. Smith
1935 - Lee Williams	1972 - J. D. Miller
1938 - D. B. Groves	1975 - R. W. Hinkle
1941 - T. W. Kemp	1980 - R. T. Wellman
1943 - A. E. Owens	1982 - L. W. Kelso
1946 - C. G. Jones	

Schools

Schools

The following information was taken from a document entitled "Schools of Londonderry Township, Bedford County, PA. The document was written in 1934 by C. E. Stuby.

Kennell School

The first school was known as the DeVore School. It was later known as the Mason School and then changed to Kennell in honor of James M. Kennell. A school house was erected near where Wilbert Shaffer lived and pupils who lived on the Creek Road attended this school until after the Shaffer School was built about 1870. Later the building was abandoned and one was built known as the Kennell School were the Hyndman Grange Hall is located. After consolidation of schools, the building was purchased and remodeled into the present grange hall. Cornelius DeVore, Jr. who was born near Cooks Mills, (1791), and lived on what is know as the "Lime Sinks." He was a strong advocate of Public Schools, and it was through his influence that the school at this place was established. Mr. DeVore was a Justice of the Peace for many years. He died in 1861, and was buried on the Shaffer Farm known as the "Lime Sinks."

Pine Grove School

A log school house was built at an early date. Later a frame was erected and known as Pine Grove. Children from as far south as the Maryland Line near Ellerslie attended this school. This building was in need of repairs many years before consolidation. The citizens wanted a new building erected on the new State Road, but in view of consolidation close at hand, the directors refused to build. While in very poor condition it was used until 1931.

Cross Roads School

A school was erected near Cooks Mills as early as 1820 and the students were taught by Michael Porter. It was probably in the Old Log Church. Just when the school house at Cross Roads was built is not known, but is thought to be about 1850 or 1860. It was quite an old building by 1900. Around the year 1916, the building was in need of repairs and the citizens wanted a new building. L. I. Stallings, of Cooks Mill, was one of the Directors. The Board of Directors decided to build a new school house. One acre of ground was purchased from J. W. Stair and a new building was erected. This building accommodated the needs until the new state road was built and Stringtown and the vicinity began to expand. This resulted in the building becoming overcrowded. The State charged the Directors to erect another building and employ 2 teachers. A building was erected on the lot purchased from J. W. Stair in 1927 at a cost of $3,300. This debt was still unpaid at the time of vote on consolidation. These two buildings were used until Nov., 1931, when schools were consolidated. In the spring of 1932, they were sold and converted into dwelling houses.

Shaffer School

A building known as the Shaffer School was located on what was known as Anthony Shaffer's Farm, now George Kennell, (1934). This accommodated all pupils on the Creek Road and Coal Tipple Hill, but in time of high water the road was often impassable. This building was erected sometime during the early 1870's.

School Expenses

Free Schools in early years were strongly opposed and only adopted by a small majority. Cornelius De-Vore Jr. was a strong advocate of Free School. James C. DeVore was one of the first and most successful teachers. In 1882, the Londonderry Township had 7 schools, 6 male and 1 female teacher. The average number of pupils in the system was 148 for a 5 month term. Wages ranged from $18 to 25 dollars per month. Total amount for one term was $1,097.61 for the Township. This did not include money for text books as parents had to furnish books and supplies for their children.

In 1934, the township spent about $18,000 for schools. In 1907, the minimum salary of $40 for Provisional Certificate and $50 for Professional went into effect. The County Superintendent's annual report for 1906 listed 11 teachers each with a salary of $35 per month for 7 months with 319 pupils.

The report of 1927 gave 10 teachers a salary of $85 and $100 per month for an 8 month term and the number of pupils at 265. A decrease of pupils in this period of 20 year period was due to a decrease in population. Also prior to 1906, and for years after, very few pupils attended high school and often attended school until they were 19 or 20 years old.

Left and Middle: These photos are a collection of old school photos from the Cooks Mill area. Identified in this photo is Emma Rae Stallings, in the back row 5th child from left and Rhoda Landis Wagus, front row 6th child from the left.

Photos courtesy of Marilynn

Below: The photo below depicts the Stringtown School group photo. This group photo includes Dorothy Hosselrode Lowery. This photo would have been taken in the 1920s.

Photo courtesy of Vernon Lowery

Left: This photo is believed to be a picture of the students from the Crossroads School

Roads and Bridges

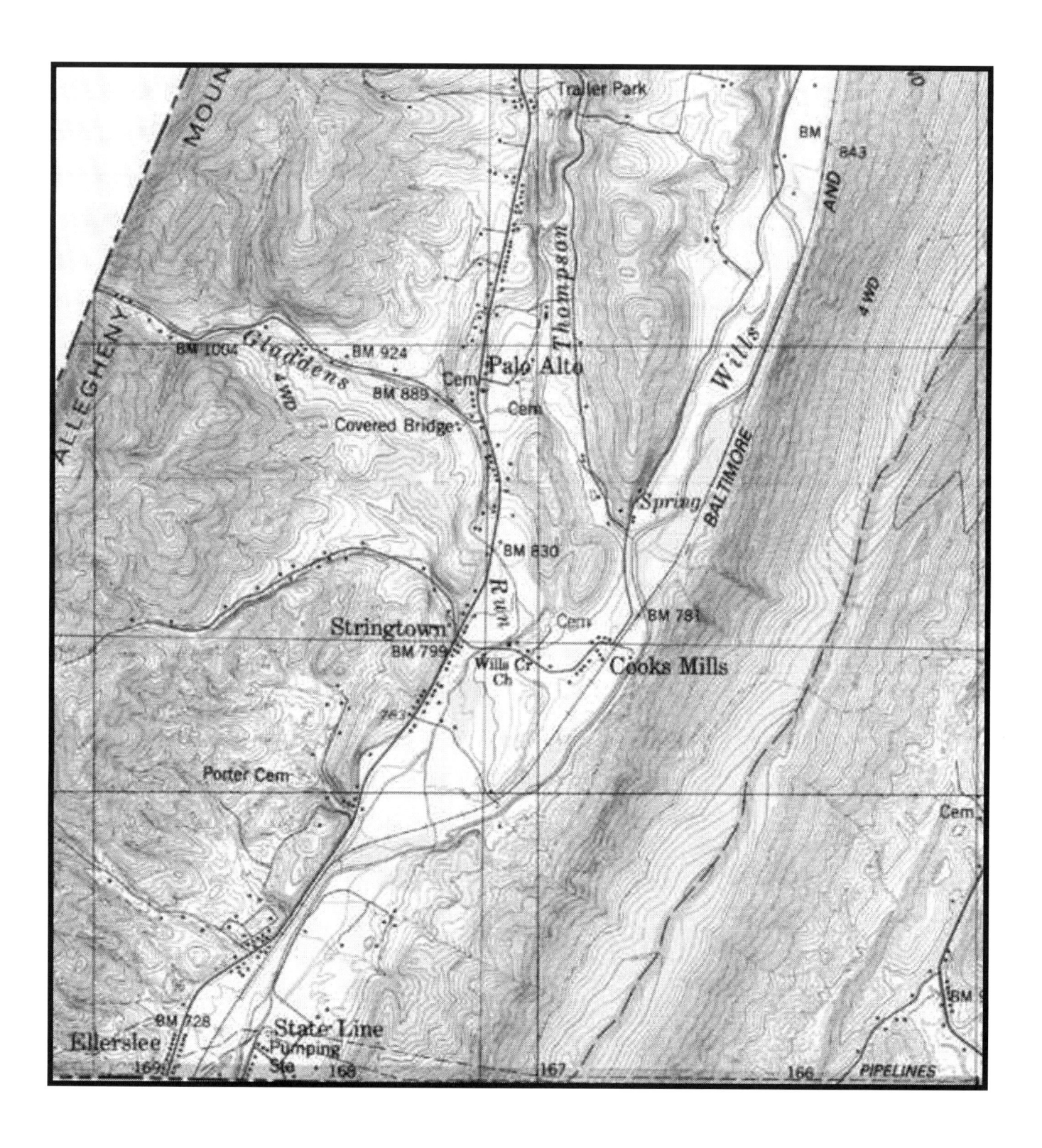

New Road Construction

Below: The following series of photographs show the construction of the new road to Hyndman, PA. These photos reflect the road construction at the Crossroads in Stringtown, PA. The new road was constructed around the 1940s. The original road went up through Stringtown Hollow and crossed the covered bridge in Kennell's Mill.

Above: The new road construction at the Crossroads continues. This photo depicts the construction of the bridge on Rt. 96 to allow the small stream from Stringtown Hollow to pass under on its way to merging with Gladdens Run. This photo would be dated in the 1940s.

Photo courtesy of Marilynn Kennell.

Cooks Mill Covered Bridge

Above: The Cooks Mill covered bridge is seen here in a photograph taken by Gary Moore in September of 1959. The bridge crossed from Stringtown, perpendicular over Gladdens Run, to Cooks Mill. Directly on the Cooks Mill side of the bridge was the ball field. As seen here, the weight limit on the bridge was very limited. Mr. Moore indicated that many of the newly constructed homes had to reroute cement delivery trucks through the Grange Hall Road as the bridge would not support the weight or height. Furthermore, the school buses would empty the students from the bus before crossing. The students would then walk across the bridge and re-board the bus on the other side. Eventually the bridge was replaced with the new concrete structure that is in place currently.

Photo courtesy of Gary Moore

COOKS MILL bridge crossed Gladdens run on route 05121 in Londonderry township. It was about 50 feet long. The Bedford Gazette of March 27, 1936 reported this bridge was damaged by the flood. When the highway was relocated, a modern cement bridge was built. The old covered bridge was torn down in the 1950's.

Bedford Gazette Feb 23, 1973

Above: This photograph shows the covered bridge that was used to cross Gladden's Run leading into Cooks Mills. The concrete two lane bridge that is presently used was constructed in 1960. The Cooks Mill Methodist Church can be seen in the background.

Photo courtesy of Edgar Stallings

Above: This photo shows the Pfeiffer house located at the Crossroads. In the background you can see the covered bridge and how the road weaved around prior to the new bridge construction. Coming off the covered bridge in Cooks Mill the ball field was directly ahead. The bridge was replaced by the newer concrete bridge and the path of the road was changed.

People

Above: Edgar and Gladys Marie (Logsdon) Stallings

Levina Burkett Speelman

Photo courtesy of Gary Moore

Above: Born June 20, 1852, Levina was the daughter of John and Sarah Burkett. She was a native of Cook's Mill and lived there her entire life. She was married first to Benjamin Kennell and after he passed, she became the wife of James Speelman. Mrs. Speelman outlived all her children. She passed away on January 8, 1944 and was buried in Cooks Mill Cemetery. During one of her last birthday parties, Levina was detailing stories of Civil War times and how the county was trying to move through very difficult times at the end of the war. She also talked of the assassination of President Lincoln.

Cornelius DeVore

Cornelius DeVore was born on March 31, 1749 in Orange County, New York. Cornelius was a veteran of the Revolutionary War. As a private he served in the Capt. Charles Taggart's Bedford County Militia Company. He would ultimately reach the rank of Captain. Following the war, he became a Justice of the Peace. In 1791, he moved to the area of Londonderry Township now known as Cooks Mill, PA.

Cornelius constructed one of the first grist mills in the area. It would later be remodeled by a Mr. Cook thus giving Cooks Mill its name. Cornelius also had a saw mill and distillery in the area. Cornelius constructed a house around 1800 along the banks of Wills Creek. The property was owned by the Deal family in and around 1968. The Brick home of the Deal family was built on the foundation of Cornelius' former home. This is now the home of Tammy Kennell. The original exterior was since bricked over however the house still shows some of the original woodwork of the DeVore era.

Cornelius DeVore would father several children to his wife Elizabeth. They included John, Isaac, Jeremiah, Hannah (Ball), Catherine (Baker), Cornelius, Samuel, and Charity (DeVore).

Cornelius and his wife were buried near the location of the Cooks Mill Methodist Church. They were originally located on top of the bluff near the church, but Wills Creek had undercut the graves and the stones had fallen down the fluff, where they had been recovered, re-cut and removed to a hillside northeast of the current church, of which the DeVore's were members.

Photo provided by Helen Lodge.

Below: These are copies of two land grants among others that Cornelius DeVore received. The first is for 150 acres on the west side of Wills Creek. The second is for 50 acres on the east side of Wills Creek. Land grants were very typical as a means to repay an individual for service to their country. These were dated August 1792. These were probably payment for Cornelius DeVore's service during the Revolutionary War serving as a Captain in the Pennsylvania Militia.

Cornelius DeVore's Will

In the name of God, Amen, I, Cornelius DeVore, Senior of the township of Londonderry in the County of Bedford and the state of Pennsylvania being of sound mind, memory and understanding, do make this my last will and testament in the manner of form following, to wit. It is my will and desire as my dear wife Elizabeth, is aged and infirm, that she might or may at her own option live with either of my two executors here in after maintain her decently during her life, and also that she may choose and keep during her life any piece or part of my furniture she may choose or wish for which said furniture after the decease of my dear wife Elizabeth shall revert to my two executors, hereinafter named, share and share alike.

Item – I give, devise and bequeath unto my eldest son John, the upper part of the sink hole land located in the name of Henry Woods containing two hundred eight one and a half acres, and half the warranted land down as far as a hickory a corner of John England's survey – on his conveying to my executors hereinafter named his right to a tract situate lying and being in Gooseberry Valley, warranted in the name of John DeVore and Andrew Russard – And it is my will and desire that my son John, his heirs or assigns or any person or persons lawfully claiming by from or under him them or any of them shall not on any fuctence whatever shut up the road or way through the aforesaid located and warranted land to and from the mountain to the mill.

Item - I give devise and bequeath to my second son Isaac, or to his heirs' $500 payable to him or to his heirs by my executors hereinafter named seven years after my decease which said sum of $500 shall be to my said son Isaac and his heirs a full share and compensation out of my property.

Item - I give devise and bequeath to my third son Jerimiah, in trust for the heirs of his body lawfully begotten, a tract of land whereon Samuel Johnson now resides containing between seventy and eight acres of patented land, and also 50 acres of land warranted in the name of Daniel DeVore, which said two tracts of land my said son Jerimiah is not at liberty to sell, rent, or mortgage, but they shall be and remain for the use and benefit of the heirs of his body, lawfully begotten, who are to have and enjoy the said two tracts of land as tenants in common after the death of my aforesaid son Jerimiah.

Item - I give devise and bequeath to my fourth son Jacob in trust for his heirs of his body, lawfully begotten, the lower part of the sink hole tract of land, located in the name of Sanders Frazer, containing 279 acres and 1/4, and also, the one half of the warranted land on a southerly course to a stone heap corner between my land and land of the heirs of Richard Baker, thence westerly course to a hickory on a survey in the name of John England, which said land so devised my aid son Isaac is not at liberty either to sell, convey or mortgage but it shall be and remain for the use of the heirs of his body, lawfully begotten who are to use and enjoy the said two tracts of land as tenants in common after the decease of my said son Jacob, and further it is my will and desire that my said son Jacob, his heirs, or assigns or any person or persons lawfully claiming pretense whatever shut up or obstruct the road from the mountain through the aforesaid here in described land on the west side of Wills Creek, nor the road from the Mountain down by Thomson's run to the Mill.

Item - I give devise and bequeath to my fifth son Cornelius, a tract of land beginning at the Spanish Oak about 25 rods below the sawmill on the west side of Wills Creek, thence north 57 degrees west 24 perches to a willow tree, thence north 31 degrees East 25 perches to a willow tree thence north 71 degrees to the mill dam thence up Wills Creek to a line between and the heirs of Richard Baker Esq including the said creek thence easterly course to the foot of Wills Mountain, thence southerly course and crossing the said creek to the place of beginning including the saw mill and grist mill and all other buildings and improvements thereon erected.

Item - I give devise and bequeath to my sixth son Samuel all that tract or parts of tracts of land beginning at the Spanish Oak about 25 rods below the Sawmill and running along with my son Cornelius' line up to the mouth of the sons run thence up the said run to a spring run including the said spring thence from the said spring upon the south said of the run at the bottom of the meadow now rented to Robert Colpson to a white oak, the hollow a corner of John England's survey from the said white oak a northerly course to the top of the ridge to a white oak from thence a westerly course to a line between my land and Phillip DeVore's land, thence upon the west side of the ride along the said line to the Wellen field from thence southerly along Phillip DeVore's line to a walnut stump from thence along Nicholas Moyers line on the easterly course to a white oak, thence along said Nicholas Moyers line to Christian Albrights Line, thence northerly course to a stone heap from thence easterly to the east side of Wills Creek to a w white oak, thence including all the land on both sides of the Creek to the place of the beginning. Together with all the singular the buildings and the improvements thereon.

Item - Having raised my grandson James DeVore and promised him $500 I have paid Philip DeVore $300 for him and I have his own for $200 more so that my executors hereinafter named are released from any trouble on his account.

Item - I give, devise, and bequest to the heirs of my oldest daughter Rachel late wife of Richard Baker ESQ $500 payable seven years after my decease.

Item - I give, devise, and bequeath to the heirs of my daughter, late wife of Henry Ball, $500 payable after my decease.

Item - I give and devise, and bequeath to the heirs of my daughter Katy, wife of Michael Baker, or his or her heirs $500 payable 8 years after my decease which said sum of $500 is to be paid and remain in the hands of my executors hereinafter named for the use of my said daughter Katy and her heirs without control or interference of him the said Michael Baker.

Item - I give, devise, and bequest to my daughter Charity, wife of Phillip DeVore, or her heirs, excepting her daughter Katy, wife of the late William Green, $300 dollars, besides what I have already given her payable 8 years after my decease which said sum of $300 to be and remain in the hands of my executors hereinafter named for the use of said daughter Charity and her heirs: except her daughter Katy who is to get no part of said devised $300: without control or interference of the said Phillip DeVore.

Item - I give devise and bequest to my daughter Catherine, wife of William Green Late, $200 payable 8 years after my decease. And furthermore, it is my will and desire that the Thomson Bottom tract, a part of England's survey together with all other tract pieces or parcels of lands not herein divided conveyed or named or which may belong to me at the time of my decease shall be and remain in the hands of my executors hereinafter named that if they have need of the money, they may sell the same to discharge or pay the several sums of money that may be due to me on the mortgages, bonds, bills, notes or otherwise get herewith all monies arising from the sale of my movable property, shall be and remain in the hands of my executors hereinafter named for the above purposes and in order my located land if it is not already done in my lifetime, and after maintaining my dear wife aforesaid decently during her lifetime, and patenting and located land aforesaid if it is not dome by myself. That then all the un- devisable land or before stated and to all monies due to me or owing from the sale of my movable property to remain in the hands of my executors hereinafter named share and share alike for their own use and benefit besides what I have already heretofore devised to them. And I hereby nominate constitute and appoint my beloved sons Cornelius DeVore Junior and Samuel DeVore executors of this my last will and testament. Hereby revoking and annulling all and every other former testaments, wills, and testament legacies, bequest and executors by me in any way before named willed bequeathed vilifying and confining this and no other to be my last will and testament.

In witness whereof I have unto it sit my hand and seal this fourteenth day of August in the year of our Lord one thousand eight hundred and twenty nine.

Signed, sealed Established, Pronounced and declared by the said Cornelius DeVore as his last will and testament in the presence of us who in his presence and in the presence of one another have here unto subscribed our names this day and year above written.

Isaac Oswald, Robert Clopton, Edward Cotter

Bedford County, PA. Be it remembered that on the first day of August A.D. 1831 I personally appeared before the subscriber Register for the probate of Wills and granting letters of Administration I and for said county, I Isaac Oswalt and Robert Clopton the witness to the forgoing instrument of writing and being duly sworn according to law did disclose an say that they were personally present and heard and saw the testator Cornelius DeVore, sign, seal, publish, pronounce, present and declare the forgoing instrument of writing as and for his last will and testament. That at the time thereof the said testator was of sound and disposing mind, memory and understand, according to the best of these deponents knowledge and belief, and they hey subscribed their names there to as witness of in the presence of the testator and at his request and that they also saw Edward Joseph Cotter subscribing his name thereto as a witness who is since dead.

Sworn and subscribed 1 August A.D. 1831

Before me Bob Mann Register

Be it remembered that on the 16th day of August A.D. 1831 Letters Testamentary were granted to Cornelius DeVore and Samuel DeVore Executors in the forgoing will of Cornelius DeVore Sen named they having been duly sworn according to law.

Bob Mann Register.

CORNELIUS DeVORE
CAPT PA MILITIA
REVOLUTIONARY WAR
MAR 31 1749   JUN 23 1831

Cornelius DeVore Jr. was the son of Cornelius and Elizabeth DeVore. He was born on July 19, 1791 and died on November 6, 1861. He was married to Elizabeth Dunlap and together they raised several children including James, Delilah, Louisa, Sarah, John, Jacob, Levi, Elizabeth, and Benjamin, Caroline, and Upton. Cornelius was a farmer as well as a Justice of the Peace as was his father. Mr. DeVore was very active in the educational system. During the early part of the 1800's education was only available to those that could pay a tuition to send their children to school. The concept of a free education was very much opposed. Cornelius was a very strong advocate for a free education system. Early records indicate that a school was underway in Cooks Mill in 1820. Cornelius' son James was one of the first and most successful teachers in the area.

Above: This is a photo of Nellie Welsh Stallings holding her son Edgar. Mrs. Stallings passed away when Edgar was five as result of complications from child birth.

Photo courtesy of Edgar Stallings

Left: Edgar Stallings voluntarily entered the US Army as a aviation cadet. Edgar was quoted as saying "Following 10 hours of flight training, the instructor got out his pad and said to me that I would be the death of both of them." Ultimately he became a navigator in the service.

Photo courtesy of Edgar Stallings

IRVING STALLINGS, one of the most enterprising and progressive young business men of Londonderry township, Bedford County, Pa., is at the present time Auditor and Clerk of the township, Postmaster at Cook's Mills, and proprietor of a well-stocked country store. He was born in Alleghany County, Maryland, January 30, 1860, the son of John H. and Anna Stallings. John H. Stallings was born, bred, and married in Alleghany County, Maryland, where he was successfully engaged in farming until 1878. Coming then to Bedford County, he purchased the store at Cook's Mills that is now owned by his son Irving. This he conducted successfully the ensuing five years, and at the same time served as Postmaster. In 1883 he sold out his entire mercantile business to his son, who has proved a worthy successor. Irving Stallings remained on the home farm in Alleghany County, Maryland, until he was eighteen years old, assisting his father in its management, and in the public schools acquiring a knowledge of the common branches of study. On coming to Londonderry with his father, he entered the store as a clerk, a position which he continued until he became its owner. The building that he occupies is a two-story frame house, the room used as the store being forty feet long and eighteen feet wide. His stock of general merchandise, valued at about five thousand dollars, includes choice and staple groceries, dry goods, hardware, fertilizers of all kinds, and agricultural implements, his endeavor being to supply as far as possible everything needed to meet the wants of his numerous customers. Mr. Stallings has been **Postmaster at Cook's Mills** since 1883, and is now serving his tenth year as Auditor and Clerk of the township. For a number of years he has likewise been the agent at Cook's Mills for the United States Express Company. Politically, he is actively identified with the Republican party; and fraternally, he is a member of the Masonic order, belonging to the lodge at Hyndman, Pa. In his religious belief he is a Methodist and a member of the church of that denomination. On October 5, 1882, Mr. Stallings married Sarah Cook, a daughter of the late John Cook, of Londonderry township. They have three children - May, John, and Carleton.

Above: The biographical sketch above details the life of Irving Stallings and his impact on Bedford County and in particular the Cook's Mill area of the county.

This information was obtained via the USGENWEB Archives and was contributed by Judy Banja.

Left: John and Florence Divelbliss

Below: Sylvia (Clark) McCoy. Sylvia married Joe McCoy and they had four children: Bill, Bob, John, and Marjorie. Bill and Bob still live on Cooks Mill Road.

Below: Duffy and Mary (Hosselrode) Mason leaving the Cooks Mill Church.

Left: Anna Clark Stair with her brother John Clark.

Photo courtesy of Anna Lee Stair

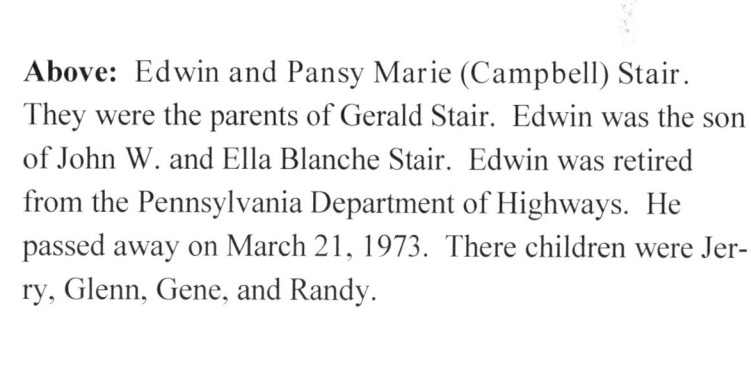

Above: Edwin and Pansy Marie (Campbell) Stair. They were the parents of Gerald Stair. Edwin was the son of John W. and Ella Blanche Stair. Edwin was retired from the Pennsylvania Department of Highways. He passed away on March 21, 1973. There children were Jerry, Glenn, Gene, and Randy.

Left: John Clark served in World War II. He was an air force mechanic and served his county in the campaign in North Africa. John was the son of George and Elenora (Stouffer) Clark. His siblings were Olin and Anna Lee.

Photos courtesy of Anna Lee Stair

Above: Mrs. Eleanora "Ella" (Stouffer) Clark

Above: Debbie, Perry, and Mary (Hosselrode) Mason.

Above: Sylvia McCoy, Anna Lee Stair, and Marjorie McCoy standing in front.

Above: Mack Wertz along with Ellerslie friend Bill Lowery

76

The Mattingly Family

Above: J. T. Mattingly

Above: Ann T. Mattingly

In 1830, James Mattingly immigrated to Bedford County from Allegany County, Maryland, and settled in Londonderry Township, on ninety acres of land purchased from Samuel DeVore. The property was called the "Myers Tract" which was slightly improved land. He farmed and also had the mercantile business and added to his farm until he had seven hundred acres. He and his wife Ann, had 15 children: William, Christopher, Samuel, Vincent, Anastasia, Francis, Peter, Jerome, John, Catharine, J. T., Henry, Rose, Margaret, and one died.

J. T. Mattingly, son of James and Ann, was born in 1836 to James and Ann Mattingly. He married Ann T. Donahue (Above Right) daughter of Thomas and Elizabeth Donahue, in 1860. Ann died in 1870 at the age of 28. In 1872, he married Rosalie Topper, daughter of Peter and Mary Topper of Somerset Co., PA., and had 4 children: Ann, Margaret, Henry T., and Agnes M. He owned his fathers farm, later known as the Stair Farm. He also owned 230 acres in Mt. Savage that he passed on to his son-in-law Joseph Mason.

Information courtesy of Roger and Mona Huffman

Above: The new highway, Route 96, took half of the Charles and Sarah Smouse house in Stringtown in 1927. Mr. Smouse worked at the Kelly Springfield in Cumberland, MD. and did the cutting job himself during his free hours. In six weeks, he eliminated a front porch, two bedrooms, living room and dining room. The house was torn down eventually, but was located across from the gas station at the crossroads in Stringtown.

Left and Right: Charles and Sarah were married at Wellersburg, PA, November 13, 1879, at the home of her parents, Mr. and Mrs. Jesse Cook. Charles, son of Peter, was born in 1856 and dying in1951. Sarah was born in 1858 dying in 1940. Their children were: Mrs. W. S. Madore, Charles Albert, Jim, Harry, Mrs. George C. Fey listed at the time of their 50th anniversary.

Information courtesy of
Roger and Mona Huffman.

Cooks Mills Cemetery

The original cemetery was located on the hillside behind the church. As years of erosion took place, the cemetery was gradually vanishing. The markers of Cornelius DeVore and his wife were relocated to their present location from the old cemetery. The burials at the old cemetery are unknown. This cemetery was previously known as the Wills Creek Cemetery.

Above: August Stair was born in Hessen, Germany. He came to the US in 1834 as an immigrant where he met his wife Maria Albright. They were married in 1850 and together they had three children that included Christian, Luvena, and John.

Below: The marker of Irving Stallings and his wife and daughter. Mr. Stallings was a prominent business man in the area operating a general store and running the post office.

Above: The above head stone marks the grave of Jesse Sturtz, a civil war veteran. Jesse served in the Ohio Infantry as a private enlisting in 1864 and serving through 1865.

Right: The grave of Jacob and Charity Witt. Jacob was a local laborer and died as result of kidney disease. He served in the Civil War with the 138th PA Volunteers in Company D.

Left: James Lowery born on March 14, 1864 and passing away on October 27, 1936. He was a son of Jesse and Rachel Burket Lowery.

Below: John Wilhelm born in 1821 and passed away in 1902. He was active in the Methodist church. He had children including Kate Wright, Mrs. David Cook, Mrs. Dr. B. V. Poole, James Wilhem, and George Wilhelm.

Left: Samuel and Elizabeth Shumaker. Samuel passed away on November 29, 1925. His wife's death was not scribed on the stone. This happened frequently when the husband passed away leaving the widow behind.

Left: This is the grave marker of John William and Mary Cook. John lived to be 88 years old. He was born in Wellersburg on March 30, 1808 and died in October 20, 1896. His wife Mary died on April 22, 1911 at the age of 86 years 8 months and 5 days. Their son Perry is also buried in Cooks Mill Cemetery.

Below: Rachel Lowery born on May 25, 1824 and died on January 12, 1901. Ms. Lowery was the daughter of Samuel B. Burket and Mary Ann Myers. She was married to Jesse Lowery. His son, Jesse Lowery, was post master of Hyndman and operated a local grist mill.

Left: The gravestone at the left marks the grave of Daniel Burley. Daniel was the son of William Burley and Katie Kerchner. Daniel was born in Cooks Mill on Jan 21, 1889. He was one of several children in the family. He, like many others, was employed as a track laborer with the B & O Railroad prior to World War I breaking out. Upon the outbreak, Daniel was drafted and assigned to the 118th Engineering unit. He was assigned to Camp Upton in New York. On September 13, 1918, a pandemic flu virus struck the camp. Over the course of 40 days, 6131 members of the camp were hospitalized. It can only be assumed that the cause of Daniel's death was from the pandemic flu. He succumbed at Camp Upton on November 8, 1918.

Right: This marker identifies the grave of William Henry Welsh. He was born on October 15, 1889. At the time of enlistment he was employed by the B & O Railroad as a Pile Driver Engineer. He enlisted on April 3, 1918 and was honorably discharged on June 12, 1919 after serving with the Pennsylvania 319th Infantry Company D. He died on October 25, 1938.

Left: This marker denotes the location of the burial site for Benjamin Buchanan and family. Mr. Buchanan was born on May 6, 1834 and would marry his wife Sarah Wilhelm on Jan 20, 1859. Together they would have 4 children including John Buchanan of Cooks Mill, and Mrs. D. W. McGregor of Hyndman.

Mr. Buchanan was a farmer his entire life and in 1859 he was called into "God's Service." He worked at the log school house at Kreigbaum's Station in Corriganville, MD. It is not clear what role in God's Service he played but he was identified as being very active in the M. E. Church.

Above: Jesse Lowery, father of prominent republican and Hyndman Post Master Jesse Lowery.

Left: William Burley, son John and Margaret Porter Burley. Mr. Burley's sister Rachel was married to Daniel DeVore. Mr. Burley is a direct descendant of Moses Porter who reportedly assisted in the in the survey of the Mason Dixon Line.

Civil War Veterans from Cooks Mill, PA

The following volunteers served during the Civil War between the years of 1861 and 1865. They have all listed addresses of Cooks Mill, PA for their records of Survivoring Soldiers, Sailors, Marines and Widows.

Josiah Cook	75th Illinois Infantry	Company A	Private
John B. Burket	76th Pennsylvania Infantry	Company E	Private
Francis L. Burket	210th Pennsylvania Volunteers	Company C	Private
Solomon Tharp	138th Pennsylvania Volunteers	Company D	Musician
Samuel Logsdon	97th Pennsylvania Infantry	Company G	Private
David Cook	138th Pennsylvania Volunteers	Company D	Private
Frank Miller	54th Pennsylvania Volunteers	Company H	Private
Jacob Brunch	93rd Pennsylvania Infantry	Company H	Private
Jacob Witt	138th Pennsylvania Volunteers	Company D	Private
Nicholas Beal	138th Pennsylvania Volunteers (Right Leg Injury)	Company D	Private
Jonathan Witt	2nd Maryland Volunteers	Company A	Private
Jesse Sturtz	80th Ohio Infantry	Company H	Private
Solomon Sturtz	9th Ohio Calvary	Company K	Private

Homes and Farms

Above: Left to right, Belmont and Ruth Wagner, Lee and Elsie Hyre, and the Phillips home including John, Hugh, Keith, Bobby, and Willa Jean Phillips.

Photo courtesy of Edgar Stallings

Left: Left to Right, Leslie Stallings, Marilyn Stallings Kennell, Jean Moats, Sylvia Ann Stallings, Betty Stallings Iames. This photo was taken in Cooks Mill below the railroad tracks.

Below: Sandy and Bill Iames, Jane Mertens, Betty Iames, Barbara and Bobby Mertens. This photo was taken below the railroad tracks in Cooks Mill on the D.F. Deal property.

Photo courtesy of Marilyn Kennell

The Smouse House

This was the home of Charles Smouse. This home is located just north of the Crossroads. This stone house has the unique characteristics of having grist mill stones installed next to each side of the front door. The house was originally constructed for Barney Deal of the Deal Power Plant family. The Deals also owned a large office building in Cumberland on Henderson Boulevard. It is currently being utilized by the Veterans Affairs Administration and it still carries the Deal name on top of it.

The Pfeiffer Home

Above: This photograph shows the George Pfeiffer home. This home was located at the Crossroads on the southeast corner. There is no date on this photograph however, it appears that Cooks Mill Road is still dirt. This may date the photo to the 1930s.

The Stair Farm

The land the Stair farm was constructed on originally belonged to Cornelius DeVore. Mr. DeVore owned much of the land from south of Hyndman to the Mason Dixon Line. He was able to get ownership of the land through land grants related to his public service. He would later pass ownership of the land to Samuel DeVore, who constructed the original house. The bricks from the home were made on the property. These bricks were used to construct the walls with the front and back walls reaching depths between 12 and 18 inches thick however the sides of the home were only a single course of brick. The roof truss to the home were half trees collected on the property. Samuel DeVore would eventually sell the home to the Mattingly family and in 1899 was sold to the Clark family. During this entire time, the farm has been a working farm. The original property ran to the Grange Hall Road. Following the death of Mr. Isaac Clark, the ownership passed to his sons Pearre and George. With Pearre earning employment with Potomac Edison in Cumberland, he would pass his half of the farm on to brother Jim and relocate to Neffsville. Jim owned the area west of the Cooks Mill Road excluding the cemetery. George owned the cemetery and the farm to the east of Cooks Mill Road. Interesting to note is that the original barn on the property set between the house and the road. The farm raised a variety of livestock including chickens, pigs, sheep, and cattle.

Stair Dairy Farm

Above: Located at the foot of Stair's Hill in Stringtown, PA, the Blue String Dairy was the local producer for milk. George Stair delivered the milk door to door in the local area. The above photo of the farm was taken in 2014 with patriotic paintings displayed.

Below: This advertisement appeared in the 1940 centennial publication for the town of Hyndman, PA.

BLUE SPRING DAIRY
MILK FROM HEALTHY CONTENTED COWS
J. W. Stair

Barns

Left: The photograph depicts the James and Johannah (Spellman) Mason barn. The farm is located two miles south of Hyndman on the Creek Road,

Right: This photograph depicts the barn of the former Benjamin and Emma Logsdon Farmhouse located on Rt. 96. The barn and the farm house are now owned by the Tinkey family.

Left: Located south of the Crossroads on Rt. 96, this barn has been a main stay for travelers for many years.

News from the Past

SEPTEMBER.—4—At Cumberland, W H. Cuppett, of Mann's Choice, had his pocket-book, containing about $2,000 in cash and $10,000 in notes, stolen. 8—Near St. Clairsville, Lawrence Imler's barn and contents were destroyed by fire. Near Hyndman, Irwin College, an employee of the B & O, was held up by tramps, who beat and robbed him. The brick mansion of Francis G. Growden, at Centreville, was destroyed by fire. 12—Near Loysburg, Herman C. Brumbaugh, aged nine years, of New Enterprise, was killed by falling from a wagon. 25—At Cook's Mills, Christopher Leydig, trackman, was struck by an engine and severely injured 27—Near Clearville, the house and barn of Samuel T. Price, with all their contents, were destroyed by fire.

January 11, 1901 Cumberland Evening Times

Members of the Buffalo Mineral company, of Somerset, Pa., are making an estimate as to the cost of a railroad from Cook's Mills, in Bedford county, to Gladdens, in Somerset county. Such a road would be an outlet for great quantities of minerals.—*Cumberland News.*

October 12, 1900 Cumberland News

John Wilhelm.

John Wilhelm, of near Cook's Mills, who died on March 5, was in his eighty-first year. The deceased was an active member of the Methodist Episcopal church for over fifty years. He is survived by his wife and five children—Mrs. Kate Wright, of Cumberland; Mrs. David Cook, of Cook's Mills; Mrs. Dr B. V. Poole, of Hyndman; James Wilhelm, of Mt. Savage, and George Wilhelm, of Palo Alto.

March 14, 1902 Cumberland Evening Times

FRUIT TREES THAT GROW INTO MONEY.

Good, clean, smooth, healthy trees of well tested varieties that bear fruit true to name.

See our authorized agents or write for prices and testimonials.

MAPLESIDE NURSERY AND FRUIT FARM,

H. C. Pfeiffer & Bro. Proprietors. Postoffice, Cook's Mills, Pa.

Agents A A Diehl, Ottown; Balt'er Snyder, Chapman's Run. B L. Mellott, Jackson Mills; Ross Drenning, Burning Bush. feb13(03)

June 19, 1903 Cumberland Evening Times

Charles Pfeiffer of Cook's Mills has been appointed carrier for a rural route recently established from Ellerslie, Md., to a point in Somerset county.

September 14, 1906 Cumberland Evening Times

DEAL BROS. MILLING CO.

Manufacturers of and Wholesale and Retail Dealers in Flour, Grain and Feed—Cor. Glen and Front Sts.—Phone 1178.—These mills were established in 1885 by Deal Brothers at Cook's Mills, Pa., moving to Cumberland in 1904 when the name was changed to its present form. The premises occupied consist of a modern three-story brick building, having a frontage of eighty feet and a depth of 200 feet, is specially constructed for milling and handling these products and is equipped with up-to-date milling machinery. Employment is given to ten experienced assistants and the trade controlled covers portions of Maryland, West Virginia, Virginia and Pennsylvania. This firm are also dealers in all kinds of grains.

PENNSYLVANIA RAILROAD
BEDFORD DIVISION and HUNTINGDON AND BROAD TOP RAILROAD.
In effect November 26, 1905.

NORTH		STATIONS.	SOUTH	
p. m.	a. m. Lv.		Ar. a. m.	p. m
1.50	8.00	CUMBERLAND	11.50	8.45
2 04	8.14	STATE LINE JC.	11 34	8.30
f 2.08	f 8.18	Cooks Mill	f 11.27	f 8.23
2.18	8.28	HYNDMAN	11 19	8 15
f 2.20	f 8.30	Wills Creek	f 11.16	f 8.13
f 2.27	f 8.37	Fossilville	f 11.11	f 8 09
f 2.32	f 8.42	Madley	f 11.07	f 8 05
f 2.37	8.47	Bard	f 11 03	f 9.00
2.41	8.51	Buffalo Mills	10 58	7 56
f 2.46	f 8.56	Sulphur Springs	f 10.51	f 7.50
2.50	9.00	Mann's Choice	10 47	7 46
f 2.55	f 9.05	Napier	f 10.40	f 7.40
f 2.59	f 9.09	Wolfsburg	f 10 36	f 7 36
3.03	9.15	BEDFORD	10 30	7.30
f 3.08	f 9.18	Cliffs	f 10 24	f 7.24
f 3.14	f 9.21	Hartley	f 10 20	f 7.20
f 3.16	f 9.26	Lutzville	f 10.18	f 7.18
f 3.20	f 9.30	Ashcom	f 10 14	f 7.14
3.25	9.35	MT. DALLAS	10.10	7. 10
3.28	9.38	Everett	10 07	7.07
f 3.36	f 9.46	Tatesville	f 9.57	6 59
f 3.46	f 9.56	Cypher	f 9.43	6 50
3 54	10.04	Hopewell	9 34	6 42
3 58	10.08	Riddlesburg	9.29	6.32
4.10	10.20 Ar.	SAXTON Lv.	9.17	6 20

Baltimore & Ohio R. R.
CUMBERLAND TO PITTSBURG

STATIONS	9	13&3	15	5	49
	P M			A M	
New York, Lv	*3 55			12 10	
Philadelphia	f5 20			7 40	
Baltimore	8 00			10 00	
Washington	9 15			11 00	
	A M	A M	A M	P M	P M
Cumberland	*2 00	16 45	10*00	3 05	*3 15
Mt. Savage Jc.		f5 55			f3 24
Ellerslie		f5 58			f3 29
Cook's Mills		7 04			f3 34
Hyndman	f2 24	7 15	10 26	note	3 43
Meyersdale		8 18	11 30	4 28	4 50
Rockwood	4 01	8 45	11 45	4 49	5 14
Connellsville	5 25	10*55	1 20	6 05	7 00
McKeesport	6 38	11 47	2 28	7 13	8 43
Pittsburg	7 15	12 20	3 00	7 45	9 25
	P M	P M	P M	P M	P M
Chicago, Ar			*7 40	9 00	
			A M	A M	

PITTSBURG TO CUMBERLAND

STATIONS	58	6	14	15
Chicago, Lv				
	A M	A M	P M	P M
Pittsburg	*6 30	8 00	*1 15	
McKeesport	7 07	8 29	1 49	
Connellsville	8 35	9 47	3 08	3 10
Rockwood	10 33	11 05	4 28	5 04
Meyersdale	11 05	11 30	4 54	5 31
Hyndman	12 01	note	r5 44	6 24
Cook's Mills	12*10			6 32
Ellerslie	12*16			6 38
Mt. Savage Jct.	12 2*			f6 43
Cumberland	12 32	12 47	6 30	6 50
	P M	P M	P M	P M
Washington Ar		4 42	11 30	11 20
Baltimore		5 50	12 25	12 25
Philadelphia		8 19	3 05	3 05
New York		10 50	5 40	5 40
		A M	A M	A M

Above: These two schedules of the Pennsylvania Railroad and the B & O Railroad ran on December 29, 1905 in the Cumberland newspapers.

Daniel F. Deal, to M. F. Reily, Londonderry Twp., property Cook's Mills $1.00

M. F. Reily to South Penn Power Co., Londonderry Twp., property Cook's Mills, $1.00.

Hyndman Electric Light Heat and Power Co., to South Penn Power Co., Londonderry Twp., property, $1.00.

May 18, 1928 Cumberland Newspaper

Miss Annie Cook

Miss Annie Cook, daughter of Charles O. and Rebecca (Lowery) Cook, died at their home at Clarksburg, W. Va., Thursday of last week. The funeral was held at Cook's Mills, where the family formerly resided, Sunday morning. She was aged about 21 years.

May 14, 1915 Cumberland Newspaper

MENTIONED IN BRIEF

Town Talk and Neighborhood Notes Tersely Told

MANY ITEMS OF INTEREST

Gleaned From Various Sources— Little Points Picked Up By Vigilant Reporters.

Reja Mason killed a large wild cat near Cook's Mills a few days ago.

August 27, 1909 Cumberland Newspaper

TEACHERS' DIRECTORY

Names and Postoffice Addresses of the Teachers of Bedford County for the Year 1908-09.

Hyndman Borough

120	H. H. Deaner,	Hyndman
121	H. C. Leydig,	Cook's Mills
122	Somers Fisher,	Hyndman
123	H. C. Mauk,	Hyndman
124	Pearl Shoemaker,	Hyndman
125	Emma Hillegass,	Hyndman
126	Alice Blair,	Hyndman

December 18, 1908 Cumberland Newspaper

Cook's Mills is expecting a business boom this summer. A standard gauge railroad will be built to the mines. A lime plant is also to be erected the machinery costing $150,000.

March 17, 1922 Cumberland Newspaper

Brakeman Met Instant Death

H. C. Robertson of Keyser, W. Va., was killed on the B. & O. R. R. near Cook's Mills Wednesday afternoon. It is supposed that he went to sleep on the tract. He was connected with the ballast train from Keyser and had been sent back to perform a flagman's duty. Frequently flagmen will lie across the track until called by the whistle of the engine. Sleep overcomes them and the train rushes down upon them before the engineer realizes what happened. Accommodation train, No. 49, which leaves Cumberland at 3 p. m., struck Robertson, killing him instantly. His body was carried to Hyndman. It was prepared for burial and taken to Cumberland where it was conveyed to Keyser. Robertson was married and has one child.

April 19, 1907 Cumberland Newspaper

MADLEY

o o

Mr. and Mrs. W. C. Corley and Mr. and Mrs. Chas. Schlosser and two children were picking huckleberries on the Mt. near Cooks Mills, Thursday.

August 10, 1928 Cumberland Newspaper

WEEK'S WRECKS

The P. R. R. Passenger train jumped the track at Mann's Choice yesterday morning but no one was hurt and not much damage done to train. There was also a wreck near Cook's Mills on the B. and O. but no one hurt One at Lutzville and below Saxton. All wrecks were lucky in that no lives were lost The B & O had a train of chickens. milk and butter; due for Baltimore, Chickens flew in all directions, so did the milk while the butter stuck to the track

July 23, 1920 Cumberland Evening Times

EMERICK — Tuesday morning Clara Marie, the three-year-old daughter of Mr. and Mrs. George Emerick, of Cook's Mills, died at the Western Maryland Hospital, Cumberland, of appendicitis. Interment was made in Comp's Cemetery, Cook's Mills, Thursday afternoon.

August 8, 1913 Cumberland Evening Times

ATTACK BY BURGLAR

At the Home of L. I. Stallings of Cook's Mills Monday Morning.

Early Monday morning a burglar entered the store of L. I. Stallings of Cook's Mills through the front door and took a Winchester rifle and several knives. He then went to the second floor and entered the bedroom of Mrs. James Hartsock, a daughter, and leveled the rifle at her, commanding her to keep quiet. He then went to the bedroom of Mr. and Mrs. Stallings and started to ransack the bureau drawers. Mrs. Stallings nudged her husband who sprang from bed and alarmed his son, Carlton, aged 19 years. They rushed at the intruder who fired at young Stallings, the bullet piercing his right ear. Then the culprit, a powerful man over six feet tall, began slashing the youth. Both father and son were weakened by the fight and the fellow fled.

As yet the police have been unable to make an arrest of any suspects for the attempted robbery. All points east and west have been wired a description of the burglar. It is thought he can be identified by bruises and marks on his face. The elder Stallings struck him repeatedly with his fist in the scuffle. He also struck him several blows with a gun, bringing blood to his nose.

In searching the rooms of the Stallings home after the struggle a loaded pistol was found. The robber is thought to have dropped it when Mr. Stallings knocked him down on a trunk.

Carlton Stallings, who was shot in the ear and stabbed in the hand by the intruder, suffers much pain from his wounds.

February 27, 1914 Cumberland Newspaper

JILTED GIRL SHOOTS HERSELF

At Her Home Near Cook's Mills— Has Chance of Recovery.

On Sunday the neighborhood of Cook's Mills, near Hyndman, was much alarmed when it became known that Miss Nellie Mason, aged 19, daughter of James H. Mason, had attempted suicide by shooting herself in the head. The facts as learned are as follows:

Miss Mason and a young man named Welsh of the same neighborhood had been lovers for some time but recently for some cause he jilted her. On Sunday a young man from Ellerslie, Md., named George Emerick, visited the Mason family and had a revolver along. The young lady learning this persuaded him to leave it on the mantel while he and her brother were taking a walk. She told them she thought they would better not take it along with them on a Sunday walk, so he placed it on the mantel till their return. While her parents were up stairs dressing to go to church they heard a shot in the parlor and hurrying down found their daughter lying on the floor unconscious. Dr. Smith of Ellerslie was quickly summoned.

Dr. Smith found that the ball struck the right frontal bone and glanced up, coming out on top of the head. The doctor says she will recover.

The girl had written a note to her mother stating in effect that she thought her days of usefulness were over and she might as well be dead. Indications are that she stood in front of the mirror and placed the weapon against her forehead.

Mr. and Mrs. Mason have raised a large family, 12 children, and they are held in high esteem by the neighbors in general.—Exchange.

June 18, 1909 Cumberland Evening Times

Cook's Mills.

One day I came up from home to Cook's Mills. Cook's Mills is a town seven miles from Cumberland along the B. and O and P. R. R. and right there comes down from the mountain the Gladden's Run branch road to haul coal from up at the new mines recently opened there. L. I. Stallings keeps store at Cook's Mills. He keeps it too. He has things piled up so that customers can hardly get in.

A Warming Place

They have a warming place for the working men at the tower at Cook's Mills. The men hardly take time to eat their dinners so anxious are they to get a seat in the tower house. They run two games and the set-backers look on. They enjoy it and forget about the war. One woman told me there was not a sinner about Cook's Mills anymore, since the church had been abandoned. She spoke kind of sarcastically but she was a woman and of course could not be contradicted. I went around the highway and stopped at Scritchfield's where I found one of the good old time women sitting in her rocker smoking. I had not seen one of these for some time. Passing there I stopped at Samuel Shoemaker's at 11 o'clock where I was invited to stay for dinner, but went over to Clark's while dinner was cooking and got invited again. They were butchering. Mrs. Clark informed me that there were just as good cooks on Wills Creek as in Cumberland Valley and she wanted to prove it. She had her way. I could not fully decide till I try it again at both places, over and over. Mr. and Mrs. Clark give their married children a Christmas gift each year of a nice fattened hog. (Wish I was one of their girls, don't you-)

October 27, 1899 Cumberland Newspaper

Mrs. Lavina Speelman

Mrs. Levina Speelman, 94 died Saturday, Jan. 8, at the home of her granddaughter, Mrs. Blanche Fatzer.

The daughter of the late John and Sarah Burkett, Mrs. Speelman was a native of Cook's Mills, near here, and has been a resident of that section all her life. She was first married to Benjamin Kennell and after his death became the wife of James Speelman, who died several years ago. She was a member of Hyndman Methodist church.

Although Mrs. Speelman has no surviving children, she leaves five grandchildren whom she reared. They are Mrs. Fatzer, Reginald Mason and Clark Mason, all of Hyndman; Clark Mason and Mrs. Minnie Campbell of Ohio. Fifteen great-grandchildren and two great-great-grandchildren also survive.

Funeral services were conducted Tuesday afternoon from the Methodist chapel at Cook's Mills by the Rev. E A. Owens and interment was in Cook's Mills cemetery.

January 14, 1944 Cumberland Evening Times

Roberts-Cook.

James B. Roberts, bookkeeper for the J. C. Orrick company, Cumberland, was united in marriage to Miss Clara V. Cook, daughter of David Cook, a wealthy farmer of near Cook's Mills, on Wednesday of last week. The wedding was solemnized at the home of the bride, Rev. Hanson, pastor of the M. E. church, Ellerslie circuit, officiating. Miss Ada Clouse, of Woodbury, was maid of honor.

January 4, 1918 Snyder's Travelette

COUPLE AT COOK'S MILL KILLED

William L. Brant, 55, dairyman of Cook's Mills, Pa., and his wife, age 54 years, were instantly killed about 2 o'clock Monday afternoon when the truck in which they were riding was struck by Baltimore and Ohio passenger train No. 23, at a Cook's Mills grade crossing, eight miles north of this city.

Mr. and Mrs. Brandt were on the front seat of a small truck, used by the former in delivering milk, when the speeding train crashed into the machine on the crossing near the Cook's Mills station.

The light truck was hurled high into the air and was demolished, while the bodies of the couple were found about 100 feet from the crossing. Both were badly mangled.

The train, bound for Pittsburgh, left this city at 1:45 o'clock yesterday afternoon and was due at Hyndman the first stop, at 2:06 o'clock. The engineer stopped the train within eight car lengths and the bodies were placed in the baggage car and removed to Hyndman at 2:30 o'clock.

The couple had left their home shortly before 2 o'clock and were enroute to Stringertown, a nearby village. The grade crossing is on a slight slope near the station and it is believed that Brandt did not observe the approaching train as he reached the tracks. The train does not stop at Cook's Mills.

January 4, 1929 Bedford Gazette

POWER COMPANY BUYS HYNDMAN AND COOKS MILLS PLANTS

Another addition in the chain of power plants controlled by the American Water Works and Electric Company, was made in the purchase by the concern of the Hyndman Electric Light, Heat and Power Company, controlled by John D. Margraft interest. The Deal Power Co., of Cooks Mills, Pa., controlled by Daniel Deal, was also bought by the same concern, which will continue to operate them in conjunction with its plants throughout Maryland, Pennsylvania, Virginia and West Virginia.

The Hyndman and Deal plants were operated by hydraulic and steam, the Hyndman plant having the hydraulic pressure to synchronize with the steam and being one of the most up-to-date plants in this section.

The American Water Works and Electric Companies operate plants in 21 counties in Maryland, Pennsylvania, Virginia and West Virginia and is constructing a $2,000,000 plant at Williamsport. Eight of its plants are hydraulicly driven on the Potomac River in West Virginia.

December 29, 1922 Cumberland Newspaper

Mrs. Philmore Lowery

Mrs. Sarah Jane Lowery, 88, wife of Philmore Lowery, died last Thursday evening at 8 o'clock at her home, Ford's Mill, Route 1, Hyndman.

She was a native of Cook's Mill, Pa., a daughter of the late Jacob and Hannah Hayman Albright. She was a member of the Reformed church, Wellersburg, Pa.

Besides her husband, she is survived by two children, William Shannon Lowery, Woodville, Pa., and Mrs. Charles Sisler, Hyndman. Four grandchildren and two great grandchildren also survive.

Funeral services were conducted Sunday afternoon in Cook's Mill chapel by the Rev. G. G. Jones and the Rev. W. J. Lloyd Interment was in Cook's Mill cemetery.

February 1, 1946 Cumberland Evening Times

John N. Burket

John N. Burket, a well known resident of this place, died at his home, West Penn Street, Saturday night, January 18. He had been a sufferer for the past several years from kidney trouble, and was able to be about until four weeks ago, when he took his bed and rapidly declined.

The deceased was born at Cook's Mills, this county, December 17, 1839, being at the time of his death aged 73 years, one month and one day. He was a son of Nicholas and Annie Zeigler Burket, both deceased. On October 29, 1861, he was united in marriage to Annie Rebecca Dobson, who with the following children survives: Nicholas F. of Cumberland, Mrs. Margaret Prince of Washington, D. C., Joseph H. and Mrs. Daniel Burket, of Black Valley; Willard of Altoona, George S., Mrs. Frank Wise and Charles R., of Bedford. He is also survived by three brothers and one sister, James Burket of Marysville, Kan.; Charles of Blue Rapids, Kan.; Lewis of Nebraska, and Mrs. Martha Lowery of Cook's Mills.

The deceased was a veteran of the Civil War, having enlisted in Company D, 138th Regt., August 26, 1862, and continued in service until the close of the conflict. For many years he was employed by the Pennsylvania Railroad Company as a section foreman, and was retired several years ago. He was a member of

January 24, 1913 Cumberland Evening Times

Members of the W. S. C. S. of the Methodist Church at Cooks Mills were guests of the Hyndman W. S. C. S. to observe the tenth anniversary of their organization. The meeting was in charge of Mrs. E. A. Shaffer, who welcomed the guests and introduced Rev. Roscoe Hall pastor of the Hyndman Church, who spoke on the work of the organization.

Mrs. W. R. Bowman, incoming president for the next year, conducted devotions. meditation was in charge of Mrs. W. T. Bateson with special music by Mrs. Grace Albright and a vocal number by Mrs. Effie Gaster. Mrs. Gaster also lighted the candles on the birthday cake, which had been prepared by the Cooks Mills' Society. A social hour followed, with delicious refreshments.

The following guests were present: Mrs. John Buchanan, Mrs. Floyd Wilson, Mrs. Mary Clites, Mrs. Nena Bohn, Mrs. Betty Harold, Mrs. Eva Harold, Mrs. Meredith Gaumer, Mrs. Nell Shaffer, Mrs. Harvey Cook, Mrs. George Clark, Mrs. Pearl Lowery, Mrs. Irene Shroyer, Mrs. Esther Kennard, Mrs. Sylvia McCoy, Mrs. Ann Cutler, Mrs. Rae Deal, Mrs. Sylvia Logue, Mrs. Caleb Allen, Mrs. Grace Albright, Mrs. A E Wagner, Mrs. Burton Rush, Mrs. Martha Phillips, Mrs. Samuel Deneen, Mrs. W. R. Bowman, Mrs. John Satzer, Mrs. Walter Snyder, Mrs. Edith Cook, Mrs. Mame Frantz, Mrs. Malinda Pyles, Mrs. Gertrude Shaffer, Mrs. Roscoe Hall, Mrs. Frank May, Mrs. Effie Gaster, Mrs. Earl Bush, Mrs. Robert Bruner, Mrs. W. T. Bateson, Jo Kennard, Annie McGregor, Mame Ake, Louise Crocker, Rev. Roscoe Hall and John G. Buchanan.

June 4, 1951 Cumberland Evening Times

Weekly Register, Volume 49   Discovery of Gypsum in the Area

Cumberland, Maryland, has long been celebrated for the beauty and abundance of its excellent coal—now about to come into "the market" by the Chesapeake and Ohio canal. It is very rich—and high expectations are entertained of it—that will be more than realized. But the "Civilian" of the 10th inst. has the following account of a new discovery that promises also to be of mighty importance to this mountain region of our state.

We have just been informed that an extensive quantity of gypsum, or *plaster of Paris*, has been discovered on the lands owned by Campbell Hendrixon and others, on Willis' creek, thirteen miles above Cumberland. Mr. H. had some of this plaster ground a year or two ago, and put on clover, and it proved quite equal to the best imported plaster in its effect. It has also been tried in various other ways, with such beneficial effect, as to render it certain of being of a superior quality. Several tons of it, we are further informed, will be ground at Mr. Cornelius Devore's mill, this winter, for further experiment. Mr. H. and others are now making preparations to work the plaster on an extensive scale. Having purchased an eligible site, they purpose the erection of a mill, &c. and there can be no doubt but their investment will prove highly valuable and profitable.

This discovery adds another to the many advantages this section of country possesses in articles of trade, which will be rendered doubly valuable when our different works of internal improvement are completed, and avenues to the different markets are opened, of which our Chesapeake and Ohio canal will afford one of the most important means of transportation.

Above: As this article reads, gypsum was discovered in the area. This was thought to be an important discovery of the time. This article was dated November, 1835. The article goes on to state how several tons will be taken to Cornelius DeVore's mill in Cooks Mill for the purpose of having it ground. It further discusses how the Henderson's plan to erect their own mill in the area to produce this product on a larger scale.

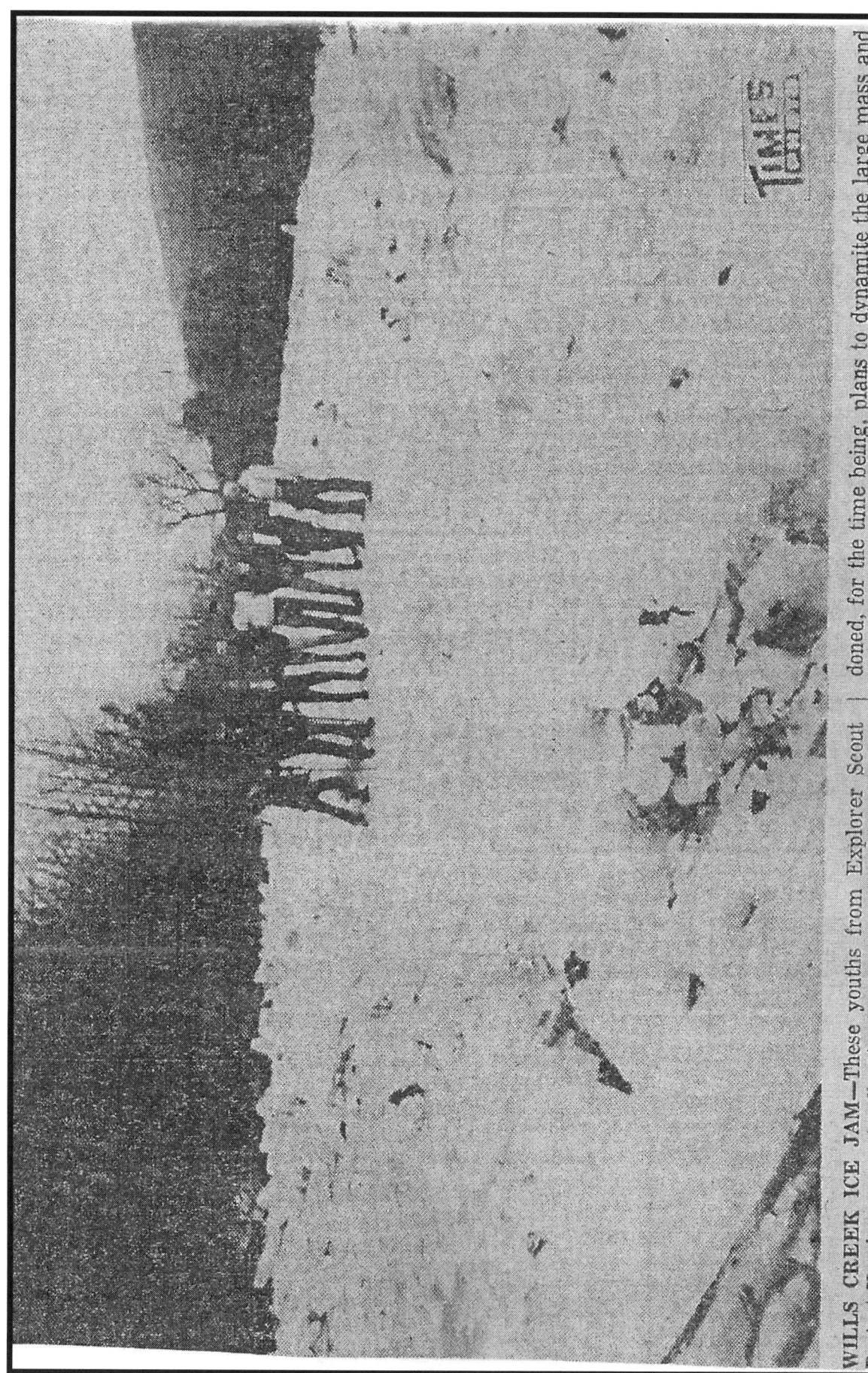

WILLS CREEK ICE JAM—These youths from Explorer Scout Post at Hyndman are standing in the center of the 1,000-foot ice jam in Wills Creek located just north of Ellerslie on the Valley Farm of Cletus Shingleton. Pennsylvania officials have abandoned, for the time being, plans to dynamite the large mass and to let nature take its course. Last week's high waters, plus the jam, caused the creek to overflow on the Creek Road which leads to Stringtown on Route 36.

SYLVIA C. McCOY

COOKS MILLS, Pa. — Sylvia Clark McCoy, 90, of Cooks Mills, Hyndman R.D., died Saturday, Jan. 9, 1999, at the Cumberland Nursing Center, Cumberland, Md.

Born May 23, 1908, in Cooks Mills, she was a daughter of the late James H. and Grace (Stair) Clark.

Mrs. McCoy is survived by three sons, James W., married to Jean (Shaffer) and Robert C., married to Paulette (Emerick), both of Cooks Mills, Hyndman R.D., and John L., married to Dorothy (Emerick), Dillsburg; a daughter, Mrs. Gerald (Marjorie M.) Shroyer, Stringtown, Hyndman R.D.; 10 grandchildren; 15 great-grandchildren; and one great-great-grandchild.

She was preceded in death by 1982 by her husband of 55 years, Joseph L. McCoy.

Mrs. McCoy was a homemaker and a member of Cooks Mills United Methodist Church.

Friends will be received at the Harvey H. Zeigler Funeral Home, Hyndman, on Sunday from 2 to 4 p.m. and from 7 to 9 p.m. Services will be conducted at the funeral home on Monday at 1 p.m. with the Rev. Roger A. Johnson, the Rev. Julie L. Applegate and the Rev. David L. Klink officiating.

Interment will be in Cooks Mills UMC Cemetery.

ARMENTA C. LOWERY

HYNDMAN, Pa. — Armenta C. Lowery, 85, of R.D. 1, Hyndman, Pa., died Friday, Sept. 9, 1994, at Laurel Crest Manor, Ebensburg, Pa.

Born Aug. 14, 1909 at Stringtown, Londonderry Township, Bedford County, she was the daughter of the late John W. and Ella Blanche (Kinton) Stair. She was also preceded in death by her husband, Alvin E. Lowery, who died Oct. 21, 1972; a son, Kenneth Lowery; three brothers, George, Rolland and Edwin Stair and two sisters, Frances Rizer and Doris Haines.

Mrs. Lowery was a member of Cooks Mills United Methodist Church.

She is survived by two sons, Darrell L. Lowery, Woodbridge, Va. and Dennis L. Lowery, New Paris, Pa.; a daughter, Marlene M. McGough, Johnstown, Pa.; a daughter-in-law, Dolores Lowery, Alexandria, Va.; a brother, Allen Stair, Brunswick, Md.; nine grandchildren and five great-grandchildren.

Friends will be received at the Harvey H. Zeigler Funeral Home, Hyndman, on Saturday from 5 to 9 p.m.

Services will be conducted at the funeral home on Sunday at 2 p.m. with the Rev. Roger A. Johnson and the Rev. Loyal W. Kelso officiating.

Interment will be in the Porter Cemetery.

JOHN I. CLARK

COOKS MILLS, Pa. — John Isaac Clark, 77, of Cooks Mills, R.D. 1, Hyndman, died Wednesday, Aug. 13, 1997, at Donahue Manor Nursing Home, Bedford.

Born Jan. 24, 1920, at Cooks Mills, he was a son of the late George E. and Elenora (Stouffer) Clark. He also was preceded in death by a daughter, Barbara L. Clark; and a brother, James O. "Pete" Clark.

Mr. Clark retired as a machinist for the Celanese Corporation of America in Cumberland, Md. He served with the U.S. Army Air Corps in North Africa and Europe during World War II. He attended Cooks Mills United Methodist Church.

Surviving are his wife, Geraldine M. (Speelman) Clark; a stepson, Gary S. Moore and wife Patricia, Springfield, Ill., and a sister, Anna Lee Stair and husband Jerry, Cooks Mills.

Friends will be received at the Harvey H. Zeigler Funeral Home, Hyndman, on Friday from 6 to 9 p.m.

Services will be conducted at the funeral home on Saturday at 10 a.m. with the Rev. Julie L. Applegate officiating.

Interment will be in Porter Cemetery near Ellerslie.

Graveside military honors will be accorded by the Fort Bedford Honor Guard.

WILLIAM DONALD WERTZ

HYNDMAN — William "Mack" Donald Wertz, 67, of RD 1, Cook's Mills, died Saturday night at the residence of his daughter, Mrs. Donna Mae Witt, in Mt. Savage.

Born October 30, 1908 in Cook's Mills, he was a son of the late William Sheldon Wertz and Mrs. Pearl Wertz Clark, of RD 1, here.

He was employed by Harold's Kitchens, and was a retired used car salesman.

Aside from his mother and daughter he also is survived by his widow, Mrs. Margaret Mae Lowery; another daughter, Mrs. Dora Louise Brandt, Ellerslie; a sister, Mrs. Sylvia McCoy, of RD 1, here; six grandchildren and two great-grandchildren.

The body is at the Zeigler Funeral Home where friends will be received today from 7 to 9 p.m. and tomorrow from 2 to 4 and 7 to 9 p.m.

Services will be conducted Wednesday at 2 p.m. at the funeral home by Rev. Robert W. Hinkle. Interment will be in Cook's Mills Cemetery.

June 19, 1976

Mrs. H. B. Altfather

Mrs. Annie Malora Altfather, wife of Herman B Altfather, of Hyndman passed away Saturday morning after an illness of two years. Before her marriage she was Miss Annie M Cook, daughter of Joseph and Martha Cook of Cook's Mills, both deceased.

Mrs. Altfather was a life-long member of the Methodist Church. She was a kind, loving wife and mother and a friend to all, always ready to do her christian duty wherever she could. She was a member of the Ladies Aid Society, The Epworth League, The Ladies' Organized Bible Class and of the Women's Christian Temperance Union. Always an active member wherever she belonged.

She is survived by her husband, H. B. Altfather, one son Roy of Uniontown and one daughter Nellie at home(one brother John Cook of Ellerslie, Md., and two sisters, Mrs. Chas. Holler of Mann's Choice and Miss Laura Cook of Ellerslie, Md.

Mrs. Altfather was born 1866, aged 58 years.

The funeral services were held at her late home by her pastor, Rev. C. A. Sadofsky. Interment in the Hyndman cemetery.

Quite a number of friends from Johnstown, Somerset, Uniontown and Charleston, W. Va. attended the funeral.

Hid Plunder Under Fodder Shock.

"Frank Francis" is in jail charged with the theft of about forty dollars' worth of goods from James Lowery at Pleasant Valley Mills, two miles from Ellerslie, Monday night. Francis (as he calls himself) had boarded at Lowery's but left on Monday night and went to Ellerslie and got some booze, and while in Clapper's barber shop let it out that he had made a haul and that it was hid under a fodder shock nearby. Samuel Albright was informed, as he was the only one having any fodder out nearby, and he with other men went to reconnoiter and found the goods and took possession and telephoned for officers and had the "gentleman" arrested. He is held for the grand jury. He says he was drunk, in defense. The goods stolen from the store consisted of shirts, drawers, gloves, spoons, shoes, hose, etc., and were valued at about $40. He had them in one of Mr. Lowery's mill sacks with his name on. A thief so ignorant disgraces the profession.—*Cumberland Times.*

Marriage licenses were granted in Cumberland this week to William Henry Hafer and Margaret Alice Howser, both of Burning Bush; Edward Lowery, of Cook's Mills, and Minnie Falknor, of Ellerslie.

John L. Feichtner to Cooks Mills Clay and Coal Co., tract in Londonderry Twp., $500.

Isaac J. Clark to Cooks Mills Clay and Coal Co., tract in Londonderry Twp., $1100.

April 21, 1922 Cumberland Newspaper

Special Thanks

A special thanks goes out to all the people that have contributed to make this book possible. Special thanks to Mr. Stallings for his gracious contribution of the Going Home! Story that is the center piece of this book about this unique little slice of America known as Cooks Mills, Pennsylvania.

Mr. Edgar Stallings

Mrs. Marilyn Kennell

Mrs. Denoma Stallings

Mrs. Anna Lee Stair

Mr. and Mrs. Gary Moore

Mr. Vernon Lowery

Mrs. Mary Kay Blank

Roger and Mona Huffman

Made in the USA
Charleston, SC
06 December 2014